D0837699

Intercultural
Marriage

Second Edition

Intercultural Marriage

Promises & Pitfalls

Dugan Romano

This edition first published by Nicholas Brealey Publishing in association with Intercultural Press in 2001.

Intercultural Press, Inc.
PO Box 700
Yarmouth, Maine 04096 USA
001-207-846-5168
Fax: 001-207-846-5181
www.interculturalpress.com

nbi

Nicholas Brealey Publishing
36 John Street
London WC1N 2AT, UK
44-207-430-0224
Fax: 44-207-404-8311
www.nbrealey-books.com

First published by Intercultural Press in 1988

© 1988, 1997, 2001 by Dugan Romano

Design and production: Patty J. Topel

All rights reserved. No part of this publication may be reproduced in any manner whatsoever without written permission from the publisher, except in the case of brief quotations embodied in critical articles or reviews.

ISBN: 1-85788-293-8

Printed in Finland

05   04   03   02   01   3   4   5   6   7

**The Library of Congress has
previously catalogued this edition as follows**

Romano, Dugan.
    Intercultural Marriage/promises and pitfalls. 2nd ed.
      p.   cm.
    Includes bibliographical references.
    ISBN 1-877864-51-X
    1. Intercountry marriage.   2. Intermarriage.   3. Intercultural communi-
cation.   I. Title.
    HQ1032.R66   1997
    306.84'6—dc21
                                     97-14597
                                        CIP

Substantial discounts on bulk quantities are available. For details, discount information, or to request a free catalogue, please contact the publishers at the addresses given above.

For Nika and for Kevin
still the best part of it all

Table of Contents

Preface to the New Edition

I have benefited since the first edition of *Intercultural Marriage: Promises and Pitfalls* from the comments of its many readers who have shared with me their own views of and feelings about the joys and challenges of these marriages. I have seen how many of the original couples I interviewed have worked their way through many of their own early misunderstandings and difficulties and, over time, have settled into a mature acceptance of one another's quirks and often maddening foibles. I also see that these couples are stronger today because of the culturally different viewpoints they faced together and managed to fuse. I have listened to young couples, who were teenagers when the book was first written, tell me about some of the new issues they face today in their own intercultural marriages. I have heard from interculturalists who help people adapt to cultural transitions and marital counselors who work with couples. And I have found that during the time which has elapsed since the first edition, my own perspective on intercultural marriage has somewhat altered.

While I am still inclined to take a realistic look at these marriages, I have an even more positive feeling about them than before. I am also more convinced that an intercultural marriage can be a sure path toward self-knowledge and growth. Learning to live with someone from a different culture, even when it involves conflict, means learning to live with ambiguity and to improvise; it means learning to tolerate irreconcilably different perspectives; it means learning to distinguish between values that are "red herrings" (one's deep-seated but noncrucial assumptions, beliefs, and behaviors) and those that are truly essential. Just grappling with the differences and running the risk of confusion regarding one's own self-concept in the process of melding with one's partner brings about personal growth. None of us who have stretched our worldview beyond its original boundaries because of an intercultural relationship can go back to being exactly what we were before. This personal growth is something which can never be taken away from those who tried, whether the marriage itself is considered a success or not.

Some very important sociological changes have also occurred since the first edition was written:

1. the ever-increasing worldwide frequency of intercultural marriages;

2. more dual-career intercultural couples, who often marry at a more mature age, perhaps living together for years before marrying;

3. an awareness of cultural differences on the part of the couples and a conscious effort to understand the implications of these differences for their marriage as well as a willingness to turn to outsiders for help in overcoming the obstacles (rather than assuming a "sink or swim" attitude);

4. greater awareness of the special issues faced by intercultural couples on the part of therapists and marriage counselors as well as the impact of their own cultural perspective on the dynamics of their intercessions;

5. a recognition on the part of same-country (domestic) couples of the many intercultural dimensions to their own marriages; and

6. an increased concern on the part of parents regarding the ever important question of how best to bring up healthy dual-culture children.

All of this has led me to revise the original book, bringing it up to date, enriching it with the wisdom of my readers, and giving consideration to the six changes above.

One of the questions I have frequently been asked by readers is why I felt it was necessary to focus on the differences. "Wouldn't it be more useful to concentrate on commonalities than differences?" they ask, "more positive to search out and build on similarities than seek out problem areas?"

While of course it is important, essential even, to focus on the positives, it must be remembered that one of the biggest positives of these marriages is the opportunity they provide for personal growth, and no one will deny that we are more likely to grow in self-understanding by wrestling with differences than relaxing in commonalities. It is also useful to recognize and acknowledge where the differences lie, understand their causes (whether personal or cultural), and address them in order to be able to move on. Exposing cultural differences and alerting couples to the potential conflicts resulting from them are ways to prepare for the inevitable misunderstandings they cause. Looking at the differences and examining possible points of conflict depersonalize or intellectualize them, enabling us to achieve a necessary detachment. Anticipating a stressful event can help defuse the reaction.

But most important, acknowledging differences can help intercultural couples comprehend the disturbing feelings of distance from one another they may experience. It may help them understand that the encounter with certain differences may cause in either or both partners a reaction, sometimes a negative reaction. It may also help them learn to respect that many differences and their reactions to them won't ever disappear. But if they can come to "...accept that even between the closest human beings, infinite distances continue to exist, a wonderful living side by side can grow up; if they succeed in loving the distance between them which makes it possible for each to see the other whole against the sky," they will have found the true secret to intercultural marriage.[1]

---

[1] Rainer Maria Rilke, *Letters* (New York: W. W. Norton, 1954).

Acknowledgments

Just as many of the couples who appear in the book have moved along to a new phase in their marriages since the first edition, this second edition itself has grown in depth and breadth. This is due in part to the feedback and comments of people who read and critiqued the first edition; in part to the painstaking efforts of everyone at Intercultural Press (especially David Hoopes and Judy Carl-Hendrick) who smoothed out the glitches and untangled my prose. I also am in debt to all the spouses I have met, interviewed, and compared notes with over the years, whose stories and thoughts about their own intercultural marriages are the backbone of the book.

In addition to the friends in Milan who were part of the early years, Barbara Cocchini, Diane Saa, Julie Gavazzi-Dunn, and Lucy ben Fadhl, I want to thank my sister Colette for her constant encouragement as well as Joan Soncini for sharing recent resources, Nancy Lemos for putting some order into my research on bicultural children, Peggy Pusch for her help with the first edition, and Sandra Finzi for being an insightful and wise sounding board during our frequent "walks and talks."

I especially want to thank Nika and Kevin for turning into such interesting and rewarding bicultural young adults.

Dugan Roman
Summer 1997

Introduction
What's It All About

The bride and groom were on their way: their bags packed, passports renewed, tickets and boarding passes ready.

The car taking them to the airport was surrounded by a few intimate friends who were jovial but, at the same time, teary-eyed and cautious in their well-wishing. There were no relatives, no parents to bless these two young people and send them on their way.

The bride, flushed and smiling through her nervousness and excitement, was struggling to control the mixed sensations of happiness and hurt which were gripping her insides and jumbling everything around.

This was really a good-bye. She was leaving these people and turning her back on her family, who disapproved of the marriage. She was crossing a bridge—not only the symbolic bridge that every bride crosses but also a physical bridge to a new life in a different country, among new people with foreign ways and tongues.

Her groom, a handsome, dark-eyed, dark-skinned recent MBA graduate, was finally beginning to relax. He was glad the ceremony—just a civil one—was over and he could escape from the ambivalence of the situation. He was anxious to return home to the familiar atmosphere of his own land and friends. For the moment he had managed to suppress the nagging fears and doubts he felt about taking this delicate, blond, blue-eyed French beauty back with him. He hoped she would win the hearts of all, just as she had won his, and that all

the protestations over this marriage to a foreign woman would sub-
side as soon as they met her.

These two young people (Yvette and Ali), one French, the other
Kuwaiti, were embarking on more than the usual matrimonial adventure: they were heading into the never-never land of intercultural
marriage.[1]

Carried away by the impetuosity of youth and half-comprehended
dreams of romance and glamour, Yvette and Ali had few doubts about
the success of their venture. They knew that their marriage might be
harder than one between people from the same background, but in
their hearts they were sure they would make it. They were confident
that love would win out over any obstacles they might encounter. For
now, all they felt were the positive aspects of their international partnership. They were proud of being different, of their daring, and excited about the adventure ahead. Only later, when the honeymoon
was over, did they realize that they had done more—much more—
than marry someone with an exotic accent.

Yvette and Ali are but two of the growing number of young people
who are crossing cultures to find lifetime partners. More and more,
people are leaving their homeland to visit, study, or work overseas.
The world is in flux, with a greater number of refugees, either willing
or coerced, settling in new lands. Once upon a time intercultural
couples were more unusual, although their history goes at least back
to biblical times.[2] However, international "love" matches are a relatively new phenomenon. Young people in the past did not have as
much opportunity to meet prospective partners from other lands as
they do now through travel, educational exchange programs, and
other direct forms of international contact. Distances are no longer
barriers. Satellite television, fax machines, computer networks, and e-
mail connect people from around the world within seconds; local
customs are giving way to an apparent uniformity. Blue jeans, Nike

---

[1] By which we mean a union of two people from diverse cultures as well as different
countries, which may also, but not necessarily, indicate differences in race and/or
religion.

[2] Ruth was a Moabitess married to a Hebrew; the Queen of Sheba married and bore
a son to Solomon.

shoes, Coca-Cola, and McDonald's are familiar to young people everywhere. The whole world shares the same threats and problems—violence, drugs, terrorism, nuclear or chemical war, AIDS, poverty, pollution—and seems to be an extended global village with only superficial differences. Everywhere the process of change is accelerating like never before. Traditional social restrictions are breaking down, creating gaps between generations and leaving some young people feeling rootless and more open to marriage with someone from a different land.

But these similarities often merely disguise the fundamental diversity in beliefs and behaviors which makes each culture unique, its people distinct.

In the early stages of all love relationships—and intercultural relationships are no exception—people are aware of and encouraged by the similarities between them. Any differences they do see are often disregarded as surface details, challenges, or aspects which make the relationship more interesting.

Only later when they get down to the business of forming a cohesive, functional family unit do they realize that many of these differences involve basic values or role definition, which significantly complicate matters. Somehow they have to be dealt with, accepted when possible, resolved when necessary, tolerated when all else fails, but not ignored. It is then that they become fully aware of how many differences there are, how deeply some are embedded, and how significant they are to their future together. Intimate relations across cultures can be plagued not only by an inability to understand each other's perspectives and by imperfect cross-cultural communication, but sometimes also by a feeling of mistrust of the other culture, something which often manifests itself when the couple is in conflict.

This is when the give-and-take that is necessary to any marriage becomes important. It is also when these couples realize that for them it is also more complicated than for people in monocultural marriages because they often don't know what or how much they should give and take, or why.

They are in new territory. Their differences are often based on expectations, assumptions, and convictions neither one had been consciously aware of having because they were there from birth and

xviii   Intercultural Marriage

had never been questioned. To oneself they were natural, and yet to the partner they were incomprehensible. Each spouse first has to learn a lot about him- or herself as an individual and as a member of a culture and then about the partner. Only then can they begin to know what to do about their differences and make them work *for* instead of *against* them.

This is a long, perhaps a lifetime, process, and many couples don't know where to begin. They don't know where culture leaves off and person begins. What they mistake for anger or indifference or cruelty may instead be cultural differences; they must begin the long process of learning to interpret one another's behavior correctly.

With this book we hope to help intercultural couples become aware of the differences and see them in perspective (both their own and their partner's) so that they can manage them to their mutual advantage. This is a book written for couples involved in a relationship or a marriage with someone from a different culture. It is for those of you who have come to see that your relationship/marriage is not exactly what you had fantasized, who have perhaps run into the first pitfalls and have begun (1) to question whether you made (or are making) the right decision, whether it is worth it or not, and (2) to wonder, "Where do we go from here?"

This book is for those couples who perhaps have had no one to turn to with their questions because they know no one who has had the same experience, for couples who feel they are alone because they married against everyone's advice and now must accept the consequences.

Until recently there has been little written on the subject (see bibliography). Such couples have had to find their own way, often groping blindly, never sure when the things which are troubling them are typical of all marriages or unique to their own because of the cultural differences.

For many of you there is no one with whom you can compare notes or share impressions of marriage because your own situation is different from others, and perhaps this differentness isolates you and sometimes intensifies your feelings of aloneness or strangeness.

With this book we hope to fill that void by (1) giving a brief overview of what makes these marriages different, special, or unique; (2)

explaining why they seem (are) harder than others; (3) showing where the potential trouble spots (problems or challenges) are for most couples; and (4) offering some suggestions for managing the differences and making them work for, rather than against, the marriage.

To do this we are using the personal stories, ideas, and advice of the hundreds of couples interviewed, some of whom have basically sound marriages, some who feel they do not, some who are still groping for the answers, and some who seem to have found them.

It is not meant to be a book with all the answers, nor one which covers every aspect of intercultural marriage, but rather a handbook which will explore the subject, pose a lot of questions for consideration, and help you find your own answers.

The first part of the book, "Daring to Be Different," focuses on some of the kinds of people who marry into other cultures. Here we consider some of the general personality types who tend to marry out of their own cultures and some of the motivations which frequently underlie their marriages.

We will outline the normal progress of these marriages, as couples pass from the "honeymoon" stage, when the atmosphere is optimistic and the emphasis is on the similarities between them, to the "settling-in" stage, when they get down to the basics of life, for instance forming their routines, projecting their future, and seeking a marital style which works for both, finally settling into a pattern which will remain more or less consistent for their life together.

The settling-in stage is when a couple really comes to grips with the many different ways in which each partner approaches life and discovers that some of their differences cause confusion and friction. This stage is the one in which the little habits of each partner must be adjusted to suit living as a couple.

For the intercultural couple this stage is often like going through culture shock or the psychological disorientation similar to that experienced by people living in foreign lands, but more severe and comprehensive because of the totality of their commitment—for them there is no "going home."

The final "life-pattern" phase is the one in which the basic pattern of the relationship becomes fixed—for better or for worse. The relational pattern is determined and usually goes unchanged unless a concerted and conscious effort is made to alter it. At this point most couples either accept, sublimate, or fight out their differences and move on...or out.

The second part of the book, "Food, Friends, and Other Frustrations," examines the trouble spots, the differences that become issues. We will look into differences which the majority of the couples interviewed felt were the most obvious or troublesome. First, we will attempt to distinguish between differences stemming from ethnic or cultural origin and those which might be common to any marriage (personality, age, social status, educational level)—often a very fine line. We will then concentrate on the cultural differences and examine each one in depth to see how and why they can cause problems in these marriages.

The third and last part the book, "Making Miracles Isn't Easy," focuses on ways of turning the differences into pluses by separating the issues from the love relationship and by seeing these issues as challenges to be managed to the couple's benefit. We'll look at different kinds of intercultural marital arrangements, how couples have worked out their particular balance of power, and how they have resolved differences.

We will also consider some of the factors for succeeding in these marriages and the conditions which must exist before the marriages can begin to function well, many of which apply to any marriage and some of which are specific to intercultural ones. Finally, we will give practical pointers which should be taken into consideration before marriage—things many couples say they wish they'd thought of early on.

Any marriage is like a game (a very serious game); but intercultural marriage is more complicated because each partner comes equipped with a different set of rules, by which we mean different values, habits and viewpoints, ways of relating to others, and strategies for negotiating differences. Until one set of "house rules" is agreed upon, the game doesn't work, and the partners risk growing apart rather than together. Deciding on whose rules to use (and deciding how to decide) can be complicated and can cause misunderstandings, conflicts, or ruptures, even for two people who love each other.

Although we may appear to have opened a Pandora's box, I feel confident that this book will serve to direct you toward appreciating that intercultural marriage, while not for the weak of spirit, can provide incomparable opportunities for experiencing not only personal expansion but for finding a love and closeness more special *because* of the extra effort it takes. By being alerted to the pitfalls, avoiding some and coping with others, I hope that each of you will find what your marriage promised…and more.

Part 1

Daring to
Be Different

1

The Whos and the Whys

Before looking at these marriages to understand why some prosper and others fail (or merely set endurance records), we must look at who the people are who cross international boundaries to find their partners. Obviously, not every person who lives and loves overseas returns with a bride or groom. And so, who does? Who are the people who "veer from the norm" in marrying interculturally? And why?

Many would answer, "Why not?" For many of the spouses, this is the obvious and logical response. Comfortable outside their own culture, perhaps born of parents whose careers took them around the world, or themselves products of a dual-culture marriage or veterans of years of cross-cultural experience either at home or abroad, they find that marrying someone from another culture is perhaps more natural than marrying someone from close to home. Others say that "culture simply was not an issue." But there are many for whom this is not the case, and others who have no international background but still find themselves first attracted, then attached, to someone from another world.

While I risk falling into the trap of categorizing or stereotyping these people or suggesting—as was the case with early studies of these kinds of marriages—that the fact of marrying outside their social group makes them less than mentally healthy, it is worth considering whether certain personality characteristics are more common than others among intercultural spouses.

Of course, there is no such thing as a fixed profile of the intercultural spouse—there are too many variables, too many unique individuals. But these marriages do often tend to be between people who are not strongly tied to their own cultures, who are perhaps less traditional or more adventuresome, and who are willing (or anxious) to venture a little further from the security and predictability of the familiar to marry across cultures.

This is not to deny or minimize the fact that behind the individual personalities there is also timing, chance, and availability...the old propinquity factor. People marry when they are ready to marry–physically, psychologically, and perhaps economically. For the most part people also marry those with whom they fall in love, but as no two individuals can agree on what the term *love* means, many rule it out as the *one and only* motivating force in marriage.

It might be interesting for each of you to think about yourself and your spouse and ask what it was beyond mere attraction that drew you into a permanent relationship with someone from another culture. Was it love only, and how does each of you define love? Or a possible combination of love and chance? Fate? A simple matter of being in the right place at the right time? Or was there something going on in your life that pushed you in a "foreign" direction? Something in particular about a person from "that" culture which appealed to you more than potential partners from your own? Perhaps similar values, goals or interests, a shared worldview?

Here are a few other questions which might assist you in discovering who you were and what was going on in your life when you entered into your marriage, which might also lead you to consider what has helped or hindered your adjustment.

1. What was it that attracted you to one another in the first place, that is, what was the most appealing characteristic about that particular individual (which was perhaps different from people you had known or dated in your own culture), and what was it that appealed to you in the idea of marrying a foreigner– romance? prestige? adventure?

2. How would you describe yourself in appearance, education, social status, economic stability, personality, and self-image at the time of the marriage? How did these compare with your partner? Were you patriotic or skeptical of feelings of national pride? Were you a joiner or a loner?

3. What was going on in your life at the time you met your future spouse: what events, situations, or changes? Was there anything which was out of the ordinary? Anything potentially stressful such as a move to a new city or country, a change in your job, or a family crisis?

4. What kind of relationships did you have at home—with parents, siblings, peers? Were you the only or oldest child of the family?[1] What was your home life like? Was belonging to a certain religion or culture or race a central issue in your family? How was this manifested? Was yours a close-knit unit in which one member's affairs or problems were taken on by the entire family, or was it a more disjointed kind of family in which each member went his or her own way and respected the independence and privacy of the others? Was this style right for you?

    Had everyone in your family (grandparents, aunts, uncles, etc.) married someone from the same ethnic, racial, or religious background? If not, how were their marriages seen by their families? Were their choices accepted or were these individuals considered black sheep? Was there anything in your life (relational, political, social, economic, or religious) you wanted to get away from or already felt distanced or alienated from?

5. How did you feel about people from other lands or about other ethnic groups within your own country, and how much exposure to them had you had? Had you lived in homogeneous neighborhoods or in neighborhoods where there were people of different cultures, races, or religions? Did you see cultures as more or less equal, or did you consider your own to be superior, or at least the one which did things in the most "natural" way, and did you tend to rate others according

---

[1] Edwin H. Friedman, Family Center, Georgetown University Medical School and Family Training, Saint Elizabeth's Hospital, Washington, D.C., found that Jews who married non-Jews were almost always the oldest sibling or only child or "triangled" child in the family. See "The Myth of the Shiksa," in *Ethnicity and Family Therapy*, by Monica McGoldrick, Joe Giordano, and John K. Pearce (New York: Guilford Press, 1966), 504-06.

to their approximation to your own standards? Had you lived, worked, or traveled outside of your own country? Was your relationship with your partner your first with someone of another culture?

6. What were your expectations regarding life with the man/ woman you married, your goals for the relationship? How did your views compare or differ from your partner's? How seriously did you discuss them? Were your partner's views compatible and, if not, how did you decide to handle them? How long had you known one another before you married?

Social psychologists say that people usually pass through three phases before making a final marital commitment: the attraction phase, the value comparison stage, and finally the role comparison stage, in which they see whether they can function in compatible roles. Did you and your partner experience all three phases, or did you leave the last one or two to deal with as issues arose?

How well did you know yourself and your own cultural heritage, and how might that have influenced your perception of the world and caused you to be in or out of sync with your partner? How well were you able to articulate the beliefs and characteristics which culturally made you what you are?

Everyone will respond to these questions differently. There are no right or wrong answers. Nor is there a typical way that people in intercultural marriages answer them, just as there is no simple explanation of why one and not another person will go into a less traditional marriage. There is no prototype for the intercultural spouse. Nevertheless, we are going to attempt to describe some of the personality tendencies of people who seem to be attracted to these marriages. While this will certainly not be either a complete or all-inclusive listing, it might interest you to see if you find yourself, or at least part of yourself, in some of the people we describe. For want of better names we are going to describe some of our intercultural spouses according to the following types:

1. Nontraditionals
2. Romantics

3. Compensators
4. Rebels
5. Internationals
6. Others

Nontraditionals

There are some people we will call "nontraditionals" because, while being a part of and accepted by their own society, they simply don't put much importance on belonging to the "ingroup." They do their own thing in life. Sometimes they are loners—by choice. They feel detached enough from their own culture or peer group to be able to decide for themselves the course of their lives.

Some never shared mainstream values and others grew away from them. Duncan, for example, was a popular young man who had been happy growing up in Portland, Oregon. He came from a solid, middle-class family and married the girl next door. It was his experience in Korea that opened the world to him. He followed his military service with college on the GI Bill, which led to a career in the Foreign Service. His wife didn't keep up with him or with the changes which came about in his goals and views on life. While he distanced himself from the environment which had bred him, she became more embedded in its values and security, and they grew apart. His hometown culture now seemed more foreign to the life he was leading than did any foreign posting. So when in Lima he met Eva, the German widow of a Peruvian race-car driver (whom she had met and married in Paris), he felt more in tune with her than he did with his wife, with whom he shared an almost identical cultural background.

Sometimes whole families become detached from the traditional ways of their society. Moroccan Mehdi and his sister Hafsa both married foreigners—he a Belgian woman and she, an American pilot her brother brought home to lunch. When asked why she had married him, she shrugged: "I don't know, but American men are nicer to their women than Moroccan men."

Others are actually happier outside their own society because they feel freed from pressures to join and to conform to values they don't fully share. Zoahar, a nonmilitant Israeli, for example, did not want to live his life involved in the political problems of his homeland. Although he was forced to serve in the military and sympathized with the emotional stance of his people, his heart was not in it, and he did not want fear and hate to condition his entire life. He felt relaxed and more in tune with Maria Clotilde, his Brazilian Carioca bride, whom he met while he was a scuba diving instructor at the Club Mediterranee in Martinique, than he ever did with any of the girls he met in the kibbutz. She neither knew nor cared much about what was going on in the Middle East, and living with her made him feel free of that world with which he did not want to identify.

Romantics

Maria Clotilde, on the other hand, was out for romance, and for her, romance meant international adventure. From the time she was a child she had been preparing herself for the day she would break away from the confines of her beloved Rio and see the world. She began at an early age to master languages and did her English homework reading the *National Geographic*. She remembers loving the lines of a Welsh poem which translated as " 'Tis better to be wrecked in distant seas than to rot in the sand of the shores." The only thing she was sure of in her future was that she would never marry a Brazilian. From there on, anything was possible. Not that there was anything wrong with Brazil or Brazilians, except that it was all "so predictable, so boring." Only with the foreigners she sought out and dated did she find the sparks, the chemistry which made life stimulating for her and made her feel special. So when she met Zoahar, she was ready.

In the same way Hans, who had been continually exposed to the international set in the cosmopolitan ski resort of St. Anton in Austria, found the women of his own culture limited and uninteresting. He dreamed of going to the United States and taking a job as a ski instructor at Copper Mountain or Aspen. He yearned to escape the humdrum routine of his mountain village. Thus, when Lynn, an American, joined his ski class one winter week, he felt he had found everything he wanted in a woman. She was attractive, wealthy, college-educated, foreign, and, most important, different from women at home. Conquering her was a feather in his cap, and it gave him the prestige of a quasi-foreigner himself. He even took to wearing cowboy hats on the slopes to accentuate this assumed connection.

Some romantics cross all boundaries—class, race, religion, age— when they marry internationally, because to them each additional difference makes the challenge and the adventure just that much more exciting. Some marry an illusion as did Esmeralda, the pampered daughter of a Spanish industrialist. She became infatuated with a Mexican mestizo soccer player she met during Carnival in Rio and married him with the idea that she was entering an exciting "primitive" world; or the English girl who married a bedouin Arab prince with visions of sheikdoms dancing in her head. Others marry as a logical continuation of their wanderlust, like the American globe-trotting professor who taught university courses to U.S. military personnel all over East Asia and finally married a South Korean woman with whom he fell in love.

Compensators

These spouses are often those who are looking for their "better half," their alter egos. Sometimes they are people who for one reason or another feel incomplete and are searching for someone to "fill the holes" in their personalities, who will "counterbalance" them in some way. They choose a partner they believe will provide them with what they covet or believe they lack.

Certainly this is not a characteristic which is exclusive to intercultural spouses. It could be said too about many people who never stray from their home culture. The difference is that the intercultural compensators for one reason or another believe that only a foreigner can give them what they need or want.

Some spouses come from families in which there has not been a truly loving, intimate relationship among its members. Occasionally they come from families where one or both parents are absent (either physically or emotionally), and they are as much attracted to the other's cultural definition of "family" as to the individual qualities of their spouse.

Cassie, a pretty, wispy young woman who met and married her "Latin lover" in Chicago, where she was working as a waitress in a fast-food restaurant, felt like the "leftover" offspring of her mother's unsuccessful first marriage. After her father abandoned the family when Cassie was twelve, her attractive, small-town, midwestern mother quickly remarried and had three children by her second husband.

Cassie always felt she was in the way in this new family unit. She saw herself as not particularly attractive: too tall and gawky by the standards of her peers, by turns moody and quarrelsome, unpopular and unsure of herself, unhappy at home, and unsuccessful in school (which she abandoned early).

Consequently, when handsome, exuberant Jaime, from Santo Domingo, walked into the restaurant one night, so obviously at ease with his group of Latin friends, she immediately fell in love with his carefree, confident ways and perhaps unconsciously hoped that some of it might rub off on her. In part she was attracted to Jaime because of his sunny personality (in contrast to her moody one), to his smooth self-confidence (in contrast to her shyness), and to the strong family ties which she felt would compensate for her own unstable family relationships. She was sure it all had to do with his Latin culture, in dramatic contrast to her "cold" Scandinavian demeanor. Marrying him was, in effect, a way of appropriating these desirable characteristics for herself. So much importance did she put on keeping ties to his family, that it was Cassie who led him to make peace with his parents, who disowned him after he married her.

Cecil, a product of nannies and British boarding schools, who barely knew his parents and had little home life as a child, was admittedly looking for a different concept of family when he formed his own. Thus he was drawn to his Japanese wife, Ikumi, as much for her strong, enmeshed family as for her delicate beauty and deferential manner. Only after they were married did he realize that she was attracted by the very opposite in him (his freedom from family ties). She was seeking independence from her strong but domineering and intrusive family. She was looking for a world in which she could put *herself* first, and for a man who would not make restrictive demands on her. She thought she had found this in Cecil.

Rashida never thought of herself as marrying to fill a void and yet her life had been one long search for identity. Rashida was the privileged, only child of wealthy, African American professionals who had done everything they could to give her entree into the white world. For most of her life she had been the only black child in white neighborhoods in Washington, D.C., practically the only black student in her class in private white schools, a token black in the elite women's college she attended. When she won a national singing competition, they sent her to study voice in Rome, where she was accepted by the foreign colony and was avidly courted by Italian men, who were as intrigued by her dark skin as by her foreignness.

For most of her life she had white friends and even dated a few white young men, but she was never really one of them. Yet she did not feel herself to be quite black either, certainly not like most of the blacks she knew. She was almost reconciled to this "oreo" identity, as she described it—black on the outside, white on the inside—and had decided that perhaps she would remain in Rome where life was less complicated for her.

Then she met Olu and was immediately attracted to this fellow foreigner with a British accent. He had a Sub-Saharan African background which she coveted and wanted to become a part of. When he asked her to return to Kenya with him, she knew she wanted to go. She wanted to be a black woman in a black world; she wanted the identity she had always felt was missing, the identity he could give her. With him she felt she could recapture her roots.

Another romantic compensator who, like most, fits into more than one category explained that she fell in love with the culture before she even met the man. Daniele was born in Belgium and met her husband, Mehdi, on a business trip. "I must have been Moroccan in another life," she mused when explaining the attraction she felt when she met and married Mehdi, who was from Casablanca. She later realized that she had only a romantic or outsider's notion of what belonging to Moroccan culture really meant, but her desire to belong to it persevered, and her enthusiasm helped her adapt.

Rebels

Cassie's Jaime, on the other hand, is what we might call a "rebel" type. Beneath his suave, easygoing manner was a young man who was disenchanted with his own country, with its politics, social mores, and way of life. Since he had begun his studies at the University of Chicago, he had decided that he really never wanted to live in his own country again.

In Cassie he found a girl who personified freedom from all the things he objected to. She was the embodiment of what he considered "American." Not only was she pretty in a natural way and forthright rather than flirty—unlike the girls from his social group in Santo Domingo—but she was free and fun and broke all the rules "nice" girls in his group in his own country wouldn't dare break, at least not openly. And she adored him, not a small matter for a lonesome student far from his homeland. Added to that was the spice of knowing that she was someone his parents wouldn't (and didn't) approve of—wrong religion, different social milieu.

These free-minded spouses are people who consciously or unconsciously marry cross-culturally almost as a form of protest against something in their own cultures which they don't like and/or want to get away from, often things which they are not able to put into words. Sometimes they are basic values or beliefs, sometimes minor or indefinable, subtle dissatisfactions.

Some are like Lynn, the suburban New York, self-styled WASP debutante, who married Hans the ski instructor. Bored with the limitations of upper-middle-class bourgeois living, she was in part attracted to him because of his blatant disregard for all the niceties which had been instilled in her since birth, and in part because she saw a way to avoid being swallowed up into the lifestyle of her parents: the country club, the Episcopalian-Junior League trap of her own world.

There are others like Helga, a true dissenter, who met and paired up with a Libyan man she met during some of the underground activities she got involved with during her student days in Munich and followed back to his own country, with a dream of working together against injustice and toward the overthrow of capitalism.

Others are idealists like Bill, who, after a stint in Sierra Leone in the Peace Corps, went to law school with the goal of dedicating his life to international human rights. To most of his friends, it seemed right in character when he married a Nigerian feminist he met during graduate school at the University of California at Berkeley. Mary was a logical choice, a strong woman who shared a belief in the causes to which he was dedicating his life.

While most young people rebel in their youth in one form or another, challenge the status quo, and then return to the fold as they age, these matrimonial rebels have made a lifelong commitment to their statements of protest.

Internationals

An increasing number of intercultural spouses come from the ranks of those who have lived outside their passport countries for much of the time they were growing up. Their parents were generally diplomats, missionaries, military personnel, academics, or international business executives. Called third-culture kids or global nomads, these young people do not feel they belong completely to any one culture, since during their formative years they were influenced so strongly by other cultures.

Massimo, for example, was the son of an Italian diplomat, who had been born in Innsbruck and grew up in Cairo, Barcelona, and London. He felt that he only knew his native Italy as a visitor when the family was on home leave or posted briefly in Rome. He spoke Spanish and English better than Italian and was fluent in French, since he had attended French schools at all of their postings. When he met Tove, who was half-Egyptian and half-Danish, it was as much the similarity of their backgrounds and world attitudes which appealed to him as it was her exotic beauty.

Tove also never felt that she belonged exclusively to any one culture, as she had been exposed equally to the beliefs, traditions, and customs of both her father's and mother's heritages as well as those of England, where she had gone to school. She always felt her future was an open book but knew that she didn't want to lose the cultural richness which defined her unique identity by marrying someone who was "limited" to one culture.

Both Tove and Massimo felt they were free spirits and had little patience with—indeed were somewhat arrogant about—what they considered the narrow-mindedness of most of their one-culture contemporaries. When they married, they created their own lifestyle, choosing bits and pieces of the things they liked best about the many cultures they had known; they raised their children without any formal religion or obligatory social mores. They felt that as a family they were world citizens, people without the dictates, limits, and prejudices of monocultural people. They were determined not to be confined by any one culture or forced to live in any one place. In fact, Massimo's decision to follow in his father's footsteps and become a member of the diplomatic corps permitted them to continue the nomadic existence he had always known and that she loved.

For other international types, an intercultural marriage is not only logical but almost obligatory. Cristina, for example, always felt that she was a person without a country. She and the rest of her family followed her father, who was a representative of Tanzania, to postings in Kenya, Spain, Switzerland, and the United States. She was a teenager when she came to the United States and, much to her parents' dismay, was quickly absorbed into the culture around her. By the time her parents returned to their native Tanzania, it was too late for Cristina to reenter what they considered their "home" culture. She was unable to accept the traditional woman's role; she did not speak Swahili, and even when she dressed in African garb, her walk gave her away as an outsider. Her parents tried to encourage her to marry a Tanzanian, but she felt that this would be impossible for her, for the woman she had become.

Consequently she decided to return to the United States for graduate school, and it was there that she met Stefan, the son of French anthropologists, who claimed he had "grown up all over the world." They were attracted by the commonality of their experience and by their status as cultural outsiders, observers of life. They felt they were really more alike than not, despite the difference in their ethnic background and skin color. "We are what we are because of the sequence of events which were our lives," they explained. "We share the same nomadic culture."

Others

While, as we have seen, most intercultural marriages are between normal, healthy people with honest, loving reasons for marrying, there are, of course, others whose goals are more calculated or self-serving, often neurotic, or even pathological. It is interesting and dismaying to note that until recently research on intercultural marriages focused on these more or less dysfunctional types.

There are marginal people who, for one reason or another, don't fit in their own society and either feel, or actually are, ostracized by it. When they fall in love and marry people from another culture, it is often an unconscious attempt to find a place where they belong or which they can dominate. On occasion they choose someone from a society whose cultural norms are more compatible with their personal norms. Sometimes they find someone who provides them with a way out of their social trap into acceptance in another society.

Some may be men or women who feel physically unattractive or are, for some reason, unpopular with the other sex in their own society, who suddenly revel in the success they have with foreign men or women.

Some belong to a minority race or ethnic group, are segregated from the majority, and hope to escape the prejudice which dominates their lives by marrying someone from a culture in which these particular prejudices don't exist.

Some people marry to improve the quality of their lives or to escape life in their own countries, as was the case with many of the war brides who followed GIs back to the United States. Some are social climbers, who marry to improve their social or economic position or to escape into what they believe will be a financially better world. Some marry to gain citizenship in another country and/or to avoid being deported. Other marriages are straightforward business arrangements and usually last as long as the objectives of both partners are being met.

These types of couples, however, are not the focus of this book. While in the past marriages across cultures seemed to be more between immigrants and nationals, wartime lovers, or international travelers, today more and more of them are between people who meet at institutions of higher learning or international associations, who belong to the upper-middle class of their country, and who have reached a similar educational level. They meet on an intellectual plane and often feel above many of the religious, racial, cultural, and gender taboos of their parents.

We have also not given much space to the role of romantic love in our discussion of intercultural marriages, although most couples will cite it as their main motive for marrying. Certainly, in one form or another, love plays a part in most such marriages but is defined differently by different cultures—something which many intercultural spouses have learned to their surprise and, often, dismay only after they are married.

In many cultures romantic love is not considered a valid or necessary motive for marriage (although universally it is the essential ingredient in the most successful ones) but is associated with eros or passion and is felt to have no important part in forming a new family. How love is expressed in the cultures may also differ. For most mainstream Americans, for example, it implies recognition of equality, mutual satisfaction, and intimate communication regarding all aspects of one another's lives. For many others, where there is more separation of gender roles, this is often not the case.

In Japan, for example, there is a form of love called *amae*, which is expressed in an inequality of sorts; one partner wishes to be pampered while the other indulges that wish. Although it is a reciprocal interdependency with partners often switching roles, it implies a vertical rather than a horizontal relationship.[2]

It is said that the essence of love is being able to cross boundaries, which usually means the boundary of ego. Few know more about crossing boundaries than the intercultural spouses who have detached themselves from the confines and the security of their own culture and bravely ventured into unknown territory with someone from a different one; who have challenged many of the norms that were infused in them from the time they were born, determining for themselves what path they will follow. In many ways intercultural

---

[2] Takeo Doi, *The Anatomy of Dependence*, trans. John Butler (Tokyo: Kodansha, 1973).

spouses are the last of the real romantics; they are people who marry against the accepted rules of good sense, who turn away from the easier road and take on the extra challenge of diversity in their intimate lives, often without the blessing of their families and friends, who risk the known for the unknown. They are people who believe in love and believe that their love will not only enable them to surmount the pitfalls and fulfill the promises of a happy life together but also help them to show others the way to a better world.

2

Phases of Adjustment

> Man's mind, once stretched by a new idea, never regains
> its original dimensions.
>
> —Oliver Wendell Holmes

No couple lives in a vacuum. Their ups and downs and the adjustment process they go through will be affected by what is going on in the world around them. This includes the attitudes of society toward the kind of marriage they've chosen as well as their own comfort level within the society in which they reside. Their relationship will also reflect the various stages in the life cycle they pass through: newly married, young parents, middle-aged parents with adolescent children or empty nests, and those retired or anticipating retirement. At the same time, there are phases through which the couple will pass as each moves from being a single individual to being in a partnership.

If you have been married for a while, try to recall various phases of your relationship—what you were like and how you acted when you first met and when you married, how you felt about the other's culturally different ways, and how this changed over time. Try to remember how and when certain attitudes and behavior patterns developed. You will be able to pinpoint some things exactly; others probably came about subtly.

Although the form, details, and timing vary with each couple and set of circumstances, most couples experience three general stages of adjustment.

1. the *honeymoon* phase, when everything new and different is a wonderful enriching gift (for our purposes we are considering this phase as beginning with the courtship and decision to marry);

2. the *settling-in* phase, when some of the differences cause major disagreements; and

3. the *life-pattern* phase, when the differences are either resolved or accepted, when a pattern of negotiation is determined or the conflicts become habits.

Phase 1: Honeymoon

Some couples know each other well when they marry and also know a great deal about each other's cultures. As a result, they are better prepared for what their joint future holds than are those who married more impulsively. Nonetheless, most intercultural couples go through all three phases before they work out which or whose ideas about how they are going to live their lives will win out.

In the beginning there is attraction. Using the words of a !Kung San woman[1] as she talked with anthropologist Marjorie Shostak: "When two people are first together, their hearts are on fire and their passion is very great. After a while, the fire cools and that's how it stays. They continue to love each other, but it's in a different way— warm and dependable."

In the honeymoon phase when couples are engaged or first married, their hearts are on fire, and while they are aware of and can perhaps even list the personal flaws of one another, they tend to dismiss or repress these perceptions and fixate on those characteristics which charm and attract them. The differences are seen as romantic, novel, and exciting. The mood of the partners is one of optimism and confidence. They feel exhilarated and approach their marriage with the enthusiasm (albeit mixed with the usual trepidation) of two people who are creating a wonderful, exotic cocktail, using all the best ingredients of their two worlds: different traditions, customs, folk-

---

[1] Marjorie Shostak, *Nisa: The Life and Words of a !Kung Woman* (New York: Random House, 1981).

lore, art, holidays, myths, food, language, music, friends. They often don't want to burst the bubble by looking too intensely at the potential problems which might arise from their ethnic or cultural differences.

Some couples, because of disapproval or renunciation by one or both families, may cling defensively to one another and their dream, and this element of ferocious loyalty only adds to the intensity of the emotion. In the beginning, the whirlwind of their romance carries them along.

Cassie and Jaime had to weather the combined obstacle of moral and financial abandonment by Jaime's family because of Cassie's pregnancy and their hasty marriage. They commented that the all-too-brief early period, which lasted till their daughter Jennifer was born, was like "playing house with musical chairs." It was confusing, dizzying, "a bit heady and crazy, but fun." For the time being they did not see or admit the problems looming before them.

Debutante Lynn and her Austrian husband, Hans, described the early days in their winter paradise as being like "a giant slalom" into which they put all their effort and energy. It was as if they had no past and the future was theirs. They never made a point of opening up to one another, of discussing any of their own deep-seated insecurities, or of confessing to family skeletons. Nor did they really talk about how they envisioned the particulars of their future together, their philosophy of life, and their secret dreams. They avoided abstract concepts and instead lived for the moment, as if discussing these things would somehow taint their happiness.

Massimo and Tove, on the other hand, who felt like kindred spirits because of the similarity of their international backgrounds, took advantage of the fact that they had been posted to Beijing, far away from everyone for the first year of their marriage, and passed the time talking "all the way back to our great-grandparents." They were amazed about how little they really knew about one another going into the marriage and felt lucky that there weren't any really bad surprises. Best of all, they were alone; there was no one else to add kindling to or interfere in their inevitable disagreements as they began to become aware of unexpected multiple differences in behavior patterns. As they depended entirely on one another for company in this difficult posting, they recalled that they "made peace fast."

For some couples the honeymoon phase lasts quite a while,[2] ending only with the intrusion of some outside circumstance or problem that puts a strain on both of them. Other couples move quite rapidly into phase 2, in which the first dichotomy between expectations (of companionship, intimacy, power sharing, gender roles) and reality appears, when many of the differences which attracted them to each other in the first place are seen as obstacles to the fulfillment of each one's personal expectations. The couple begins to see what really *is* different and to realize what the differences mean for their lives together.

Phase 2: Settling In

As the novelty of the marriage wears off and some of the politeness and careful behavior between the spouses are shed, the partners begin to fall back into old habits and manners and expose sides of themselves, both personal and cultural, which, while not necessarily hidden, were not obvious or given much importance before. This is the phase when each partner expects to settle into his or her own culturally preconceived notion of married life, of the roles of wife and husband. It is the period when each gets the first inkling that perhaps the partner's conception of these roles is different and is going to affect how they fulfill them.

Anne E. Imamura, in her study of foreign wives of Nigerians, uses the term *role expectation* to refer to "the perception each spouse has of his or her own role and the role of the spouse." She says that "few actual roles may be visible during courtship. Mate selection, then, follows role anticipation. As actual roles come to differ from anticipated, accommodation takes place or the marriage dissolves."[3] In other

---

[2] Psychologist Dorothy Tennov concluded that the average duration of what she calls "limerence," or romantic love, is between eighteen months and three years. Dorothy Tennov, *Love and Limerence: The Experience of Being in Love* (New York, Stein and Day, 1979).

[3] Anne E. Imamura, "Husband-Wife Role Misunderstanding: The Case of International Marriage," *International Journal of Sociology of the Family* 16 (Spring 1986): 39.

words, how well each partner adjusts his or her expectations to what is possible will determine how seamlessly this second phase will proceed.

This period marks the "digging-in" phase of marriage as much as the settling-in one, when both spouses begin defending their own "right ways" against foreign assault and when their differing notions about life and marriage surface. It is often at this point that the first strains are put on the marriage and the adage "exotic is erotic" changes to "exotic is exasperating." Words and phrases couples use to describe this phase are "the loudest," "full of friction and misunderstandings," a time of "fights and hurt feelings."

When the ski season ended, the honeymoon was over for Lynn and Hans. Lynn remembers feeling both afraid and guilty when she experienced the first shadows of discontent, which she attributed to the gloomy weather during the "rain and mud season" and the slow pace of life. There was no doubt in her mind that she still loved her handsome husband (though he didn't look quite as dashing out of his ski instructor's jumpsuit and sunglasses, and he didn't bathe quite as often as she would have liked).

The beauties of the landscape surrounding St. Anton still awed her, but the walls of their tiny apartment seemed to have closed in on her as the snow turned to rain and the streets outside to slush. As the hotels and restaurants shut down one by one and the tourists departed, Hans took to spending long hours with his fellow instructors, drinking in the corner *Gasthaus* to while away the time until the summer mountain climbing season began, leaving Lynn to her own devices.

Lynn found she didn't have enough books in English to read; she missed having a girlfriend she could really talk to—the women there seemed different. There was no one she could confide in or do things with or share her new impressions with, who would really understand where she was coming from. She didn't know what to do with herself in this rural setting. She was a city girl struggling with a new environment and a new relationship; she had the "outsider blues."

She sensed that Hans might be having second thoughts about their impulsive marriage. He seemed to be fussing at her all the time, trying to transform her into a typical hausfrau, precisely what he had always said he didn't want. He had claimed that he chose to marry her *because* she was different, but he seemed to want her to be different in just some ways, the ways he liked, but not in others.

Hans, who had automatically returned to his old routines, bristled under Lynn's complaints about the time he spent away from her with his friends. He wasn't about to let her become one of those domineering American wives he had heard about. She was just going to have to learn how things were done here; she wasn't in America anymore. He became conscious of the fact that she didn't know how to run a house or shop well in the marketplace, that she always had her nose in a book (in English to boot), that she didn't make friends with the other women, and that she complained about being alone and about the heating in the apartment (instead of dressing properly for the cold) and about not having enough to do. They collected little gripes about one another, which began to strain their tolerance, tarnishing the glow of their relationship.

Cassie and Jaime had very little time to honeymoon before morning sickness and reality set in. Then Jennifer was born and Cassie had to quit work and stay home to care for the baby. There were no grandparents or relatives to help out and Jaime (whose parents had cut off his allowance) had to quit school and find a job to support his new family, something which was easier said than done without proper papers or fluency in English. He knew he would have his papers eventually, the "green card" which would permit him to stay and work, but that took time; they needed money now!

At first he was disbelieving, then frustrated and angry as he was turned down at place after place, despite his years of college and his privileged background. Finally he found a job as a short-order cook in Cassie's old restaurant, at a salary which was less than he had previously received as an allowance from his parents for himself alone.

Jaime was demoralized at having to perform manual labor, his masculinity offended. Overnight he seemed to change from a carefree, optimistic young man to a demanding, impatient despot. He began asserting his authority in "funny little ways," according to Cassie, to show he was the man at home that he was prevented from being in the outside world.

He berated Cassie for her irresponsible, disorderly ways and criticized her friends, complaining that she saw too much of them. He wanted her at home, alone with the baby, being a mother full time. He wanted her to cook his national dishes, to learn his language, and to dress like a señora.

Both these couples were deep into the settling-in phase before they knew what was happening. Suddenly they became aware that not only were their personalities different, but their culturally based ideas about life, spousal roles, and correct behavior were also in contrast.

In phase 2 cultural variants are no longer simply different accents or physical characteristics, but basic realities which are expressed in questions such as, "Why shouldn't a woman go out alone?" "Who is changing the diapers?" "Do *you people* always yell when you talk?" "Must we always have a brother/cousin/friend living with us?" The differences become perplexing, some of them irritants, others alarming.

When couples begin to hew out a routine for their lives, they become more aware of the impact of the differences than the similarities. The differences suddenly seem more negative than positive, and the negative differences appear bigger, more ominous, and overwhelming. Love begins to take a back seat to compatibility.

In the book *Sex in America* the authors note the strong incentives for people to date and marry others like themselves: "Likes attract each other because the partnerships between similar people work best.... Not only do the man and woman in a partnership have sex together, but they share conversations and meals, they decide which movie to see on a Saturday night and which radio station to listen to when they drive there. The more alike the individuals are, the easier it is to share their lives."[4]

The old saying states, "Similarity leads to compatibility, dissimilarity to incompatibility." The more differences there are and the more severe, the more difficult it is for a couple to live compatibly.

---

[4]   Robert T. Michael, John H. Gagnon, Edward O. Laumann, and Gina Kolata, *Sex in America* (Boston: Little Brown, 1994), 54.

In phase 2, the couples are learning what they do and don't have in common, how alike or dissimilar they really are. Generally wanting to continue being together, they also want to continue having and doing the things they like, and they want the other to share their tastes. Some fortunate ones, who were originally attracted by their similarity of interests as well as viewpoints, find that these shared interests are what keep them going despite their many dissimilarities. But others discover that they are worlds apart. And so there are choices and compromises to be made, and most difficult of all, sometimes even their styles of reaching these compromises may be quite different.

Of course, being different and having different viewpoints and interests is not always a problem. In fact, many couples would argue that being similar is too predictable and, in the end, dull. They maintain that what keeps life interesting for them is the challenge of continuous discovery, the possibility of reshaping their own perspective as a result of encountering their partner's. Then too, some differences are complementary; they are good for harmony and balance. A moody person may benefit from association with a carefree one, and a person bred in a demonstrative culture may gain patience living with someone from a more reflective one. Some differences are enriching, exposing alternative ways of resolving problems. Some, while not complementary, are compatible in that they don't conflict with or obstruct the other: the artist and the scientist may have dissimilar interests and ways of looking at life, but they are not mutually exclusive.

Other differences, unfortunately, increase disharmony, especially when they are numerous or extreme or when the marriage is under strain for other reasons. Then differences can become intolerable and cause ruptures. When the strain reaches the crisis point in an intercultural marriage, the couple generally focuses on the cultural differences, often exaggerating these and blaming them for every problem.

Why is this? One reason is that cultural differences are easy to spot. People often don't know what they are fighting about and grope around to find something obvious. Sometimes the real reasons for the strained marriages are too deep to be seen clearly or too sensitive for the couple to face, and cultural difference is an easy target.

Cassie's ways were different from those of Jaime's mother and sister (who were his closest examples of what women should be), and so he attacked her ways as being unfeminine. He blamed Cassie for his angry flare-ups instead of facing what was really bothering him: his fears and frustrations as a new father, principal wage earner, and illegal alien. Her "American feminist" behavior was different from his culturally bred expectations and thus became a scapegoat for his true problems.

In some cases, however, people have simply married the wrong partner, not the wrong culture, and can't accept or understand that cultural differences have little or nothing to do with their real problems. When they run into the first snags in the relationship, instead of admitting they might have made the wrong choice, they make culture the culprit.

Sensation-seeking Esmeralda and her Mexican soccer star, who had no valid basis for their marriage, cited, respectively, "Spanish arrogance" and "Mexican primitiveness" for the failure of their marriage. They talked in stereotypes. Both refused to face up to their personal deficiencies, their educational and social disparity which, combined with their cultural differences, made their union an impossible one from the very start.

There is no doubt that intercultural marriages take more effort than other marriages because there are so many more elements to be blended, the differences are more dramatic, and the partners may have totally disparate ways of solving problems. Some people are simply not prepared to make that extra effort. They are mired in their ethnocentric positions, refusing or unable to budge from familiar viewpoints (which they often call principles), and then use the differences in culture as an excuse. They fall back on stereotypes: "He is just too Chinese/Greek/German to understand." "It's no use." "I'm an Italian/American/Senegalese and we don't do/put up with this/that," and so on. Anything different is wrong or inferior and, therefore, the cause of the problems.

But at the same time, there is no doubt that cultural differences count; there are some which do indeed jeopardize marital compatibility and threaten marital success. This holds true, especially, for the differences which have to do with ways of relating (showing love and caring), communicating, and reacting to stressful events.[5]

Milee, a Vietnamese war bride, spoke of wrapping herself into a silent knot in reaction to the fear and loneliness she experienced upon arriving in her new country. She felt insecure and abandoned by her gregarious Australian husband, Harry, who in turn misread her behavior as antisocial and antagonistic toward his friends and homeland.

Instead of responding to her unspoken cry for reassurance and companionship, he reacted by taking on more out-of-town assignments and spending his home time more and more with his drinking buddies, whom Milee then came to resent as intruders who were taking her husband away from her. This cycle of hurt, accusations, and resentment continued to build. Neither of them knew what to do.

Harry didn't understand that she couldn't verbally express to him her inner feelings, that she expected him to be able to intuit them if he loved her; and Milee didn't understand that he was escaping from what he saw as her silent hostility toward him. Only when they found help from a third party, who was familiar with both cultures, were they able to unravel the skein of misunderstandings.

Problems of this kind often involve multiple aspects. On one front it is a question of *communication*. People often don't understand each other's messages because they have different ways of sending and receiving them (a problem common to all marriages, especially in the early stages, but complicated by the difference of language and the culturally different ways of expressing emotion). On another front it is the degree to which each has a *sensitivity* to and appreciation for the other's different needs—needs which are possibly not shared. An emotional response to stressful situations may be not only culturally different, but culturally conflicting as well as mutually antagonizing.

Often the couple has arrived at an intellectual understanding of the other's culture, but true emotional empathy eludes them. Although

---

[5] Stressful events can be defined as those that push us beyond a normal neutral state—events such as a death, a birth, relocations, and changes in status and/or style of living. Stress is the response of the body to the demands on it for adaptation or adjustment to the event. Some life passages which couples cite as especially difficult are guiding children through adolescence or facing the empty nest or retirement.

British Cecil learned to understand that his freedom-seeking Japanese wife giggled when she was upset or frightened, he could not relate to it, just as Ikumi couldn't reconcile herself to the fact that when Cecil was upset, he exploded. Each resented the other's way and responded inappropriately. Understanding was not enough; both had to learn to allow for the other's differentness, expect it, and *practice not reacting* to it from their own cultural viewpoint. It took years for Ikumi to stop, remind herself that Cecil was just doing his "Western thing," and not recoil when he blew up.

Even after intercultural couples are well past the settling-in phase, some (or many) of their differences may crop up again and again as trouble spots in their continuous effort to find the right fit for their different personalities and different cultures. These trouble spots are the focus of Part 2.

Phase 3: Life Patterns

What happens at this point in the marriage depends entirely on the particular couple. Some end the marriage, having decided that their differences are insurmountable. While many intercultural couples believe that their marriage actually has a greater potential for success than a monocultural one and work diligently until they iron out the problem areas, others never manage to reconcile their differences, and their marriages end in separation or divorce.[6] Some resolve their difficulties by habitually fighting them out, usually from their original starting point, and continue doing so, time after time, until the end of their marriage (or their lives). As one American wife of a Japanese put it, "I rant and rave and screech and he gives me the silent treatment. When we get tired of it all, we make love and that's that. Nothing's solved, but it no longer seems that important...until the next time it comes up." They never really resolve anything; they simply streamline

---

[6] Although there are no reliable data for the success or failure of intercultural marriages worldwide, data on marriages in general show that the greatest number of separations, if they are going to occur at all, will take place around the fourth year. Helen E. Fisher, *Anatomy of Love: A Natural History of Mating, Marriage and Why We Stray* (New York: Fawcett Columbine, 1992).

their fighting methods. This then becomes their way of handling their differences.

Others turn their back on the issues. They try to ignore them and pretend they don't exist. Neither partner is converted to the other's point of view and, knowing that discussion about the problem will always end in a fight, choose to ignore it. Some choose to live loosely connected, separate lives. The issue of their separateness or repressed, unresolved disagreements seethes beneath the surface of their relationship but is never permitted to explode. Many consider this a resolution because they are convinced that there is no other answer for them. Exploring the issues always leads to a fight.[7]

Another related way couples deal with problematic differences is to sublimate them and concentrate on the advantages of the relationship, the superior qualities of the spouse, the pluses of the other culture which perhaps outnumber or override the negatives. They change their focus; they learn over time to heed missing elements less (even things which once seemed important to them) and to value what they have gained through their marriage. As the same American woman who fought and then forgot her gripes with her Japanese husband said, "I try to remember how much safer I've always felt here in comparison to the crime-ridden cities of the U.S. I keep telling myself that I am bringing my children up in a culture which teaches traditional moral values. Sure, I miss having a husband who is a real companion, but at least he's still around—unlike many of my friends back home caught up in the 'Me movement,' who are divorced and living alone."

The couples whom psychologists like to call their "dream couples" are, however, the ones who know and accept that their marriages are lifetime negotiations. "It never stops" is how one German husband puts it. "My Pakistani wife and I are a veritable UN. We never seem to

---

[7] According to research by psychologists at the University of California, Berkeley, and the University of Washington, it is not the inevitable differences which doom marriages, but rather the way in which the couples fight them out—whether or not their fighting styles are similar or compatible and whether or not there are at least five times as many kind and loving moments as there are instances of anger, contempt, or disgust. Anthony Schmitz, "The Secret to a Good Marriage," *Health*, (March/April 1995).

make much progress, because there are always new things to work out, but we are getting better and better at bartering and knowing from the start that we have to modify our positions if we are to resolve anything."

Many of these couples also report that as time goes on, it becomes easier. They learn to get beyond the minor clashes, to discuss things which were difficult to verbalize at first, and therefore to understand (or to resign themselves to) what is behind the other's position, even though they may not understand it.

These couples are usually the ones who, over time, also learn to laugh at many of the less than life-shattering differences and accept the fact that they are never going to convert one another or see everything the same way, and that's all right too.

In Part 3 we will examine some different life patterns that couples tend to fall into, and see how some manage the issues involved.

Part 2

Food, Friends, and Other Frustrations

Not all differences cause problems for intercultural couples, and even those which easily can and often do, don't cause problems for everyone. Making a definitive list of potential pitfalls is a problem. Not only is the personality mixture different for each couple, as it is in all marriages, but in intercultural marriages there are inexhaustible possibilities for multiple mixtures of cultural values, assumptions, and beliefs; religion; ethnicity; and educational and social background.

However, there are enough areas which are continually cited as trouble spots by intercultural couples to make it possible to draw up a list of potential pitfalls. Obviously, those reading this book will have their own list of intercultural challenges, some of which will match the ones listed here, others which will be missing. But almost all the couples interviewed for this book agreed that the areas listed below could cause disagreements for intercultural partners.

As noted earlier, some people object to any list of challenges, feeling that it is more constructive to concentrate on commonalities. While there is a certain truth to this, at the same time it is a bit naive to pretend that the hurdles are not there simply because one does not look at them. In most cases they do exist, and when they do, a couple must be able to recognize and identify them in order to make progress toward managing them. It is extremely helpful to be exposed to the possible cultural "why-for" behind a partner's behavior or point of view. Knowing that there are differences that might possibly be cultural rather than individual, the couple can get some distance from them and so learn to work at exploring rather than personalizing the perceived wrongs.

It is important to remember that we are merely presenting the issues in Part 2, whereas in Part 3 we will offer some practical solutions. However, bear in mind that while many of the issues are shared to some degree by most of the couples, the resolution of each is a purely personal matter, depending on the makeup and personal investment of each individual couple in resolving them.

Here is our list of potential trouble spots for intercultural marriages.

1. Values
2. Food and Drink
3. Sex
4. Male-Female Roles

5. Time

6. Place of Residence

7. Politics

8. Friends

9. Finances

10. In-laws

11. Social Class

12. Religion

13. Raising Children

14. Language and Communication

15. Responding to Stress and Conflict

16. Illness and Suffering

17. Ethnocentrism

18. The Expatriate Spouse

19. Coping with Death or Divorce

Some issues overlap somewhat (sex and male-female roles, for example, or religion and values), but there are also important distinctions between them, thus they merit separate discussion. Some may seem trivial, such as food or time, but married life is made up of day-to-day trivia, and underlying the apparent trivia, there are deeply rooted personal or cultural values.

Most of these areas are potentially problematic to all marriages, not just to intercultural ones. However, it is the degree to which they exist which is not the same. In intercultural marriages the differences are often extreme or more dramatic. They involve cultural identity and thereby are unconscious and more difficult to resolve. And the more different the cultures, the more difficult the job.

Some couples insist that cultural differences are not issues at all (if two people are truly in love, etc., etc.). This does not mean they are not issues. It usually means that these couples haven't thought about or don't see these differences as cultural issues, that they didn't cause the couple problems, that the couple has somehow managed to overcome or resolve these areas of difference without being aware of what they were doing, or that in their particular personal/cultural mix, certain differences were unimportant or even nonexistent. Or it may mean that they had so much else going for them in common interests, goals, and complementary personalities that they simply slid past the cultural hurdles. But generally speaking, cultural differences do indeed exist, and many pose challenges for the intercultural couple.

Let's look at the issues, one by one, and see how they often become problems.

3

Values

Man is the only animal that laughs and weeps; for he is the
only animal that is struck with the difference between what
things are and what they ought to be.
                                    —William Hazlitt, *Table Talk*

We begin our discussion with values because they are central to virtually everything. That which means enough to become an issue in an intercultural marriage emerges from a value, whether we know it or intend it to or not.

It can usually be said that when couples are in conflict, it is because they are operating from within two different value systems that are not in agreement. Couples with similar values generally have a greater chance of marital compatibility, no matter what their cultural differences may be. The problem is that many couples have similar values in some domains but not in others, which they may not realize until they are well into the marriage.

Values are the great intangible. People speak of the importance of having the same values in marriage but become tongue-tied when it comes to expressing just what their own values are. They often recognize what values or beliefs they hold dear only when one of these has been stepped on.

The word *value* comes from the Latin *valere*, which means "to be worth." In fact, as we use the term, *values* indicates what matters, what is seen as good and bad, right and wrong, true and false, important and unimportant. Values tell us much about who we are, what we believe in, and how we will behave and evaluate behavior.

Values are taught in the home, often unconsciously, and reinforced by society; so we can say that values are generally culturally
determined. They are, to use the words of Raymonde Carroll, a Tuni-
sian-born French woman married to an American, the result of everything we have learned from the moment of our birth, including
"...the gestures, the words, and the care of those who surrounded
[us];...the noises, the colors, the smells, the body contact;...the way
[we were] raised, rewarded, punished, held, touched, washed, fed...."
As she says, "culture is the logic by which [we] give order to the world."[1]

The ancient Greek philosophers Aristotle and Plato said that human beings desire real goods and apparent goods. Simplistically put,
real goods are things we *need*; apparent goods are things we *want*.
Needs are biological, inherent, or natural (we are born with them)
and universal, but often unconscious. Wants are acquired (bred into
us by environment, circumstances); they are individual and conscious
(we generally know what we want).

People of different cultures, while having the same fundamental
needs (eating, sleeping, procreating, etc.), may very well have not only
quite different wants (social and psychological) but also quite different ways of perceiving their needs. Both are convinced of the "rightness" of their ways, because they are behaving instinctively, naturally,
and properly according to their own cultural logic. There is potential
for conflict because what is natural for one is not always natural for
the other. Their divergence is further complicated by the fact that many,
if not most, of their behavior patterns are based on unconscious values and cultural assumptions about how life should be lived. They
have "learned to breathe [their cultural] logic and to forget that they
had learned it."[2]

Psychologist Edward C. Stewart and coauthor Milton J. Bennett
in *American Cultural Patterns*[3] offer a model for better understanding
the nature of these assumptions and values and how they vary from
culture to culture.

---

[1] Raymonde Carroll, *Cultural Misunderstandings: The French-American Experience*
(Chicago: University of Chicago Press, 1988), 3.

[2] Ibid.

[3] Edward C. Stewart and Milton J. Bennett, *American Cultural Patterns: A Cross-Cultural Perspective* (Yarmouth, ME: Intercultural Press, 1991), 66 ff.

The authors divide cultural values and assumptions into four components, which they then analyze from a cross-cultural perspective: (1) form of activity, (2) form of relations to others, (3) perception of the world, and (4) perception of the self.[4]

Under "form of activity" they compare the American orientation toward "doing" (working as an active way of forming the future, making and being responsible for one's own decisions, etc.) with the orientation of other cultures in which "being" is the predominant value (living for and making the most of, or enjoying, the present), and with still others which are oriented toward "being-in-becoming" or self-growth.

Under "form of relations to others" they compare the American orientation toward interpersonal equality (with easily established, informal, but relatively impermanent relationships) with the status-conscious, formal, longer-lasting, and involved relationships common to many other cultures.

Under "perception of the world" they compare the ways different cultures consider humankind's relationship to nature (Americans see humans as separate from nature, while many other cultures see humans as an integral part of it) and show how they deal with the world around them (exploiting it for their own needs versus respecting or fearing it as a force beyond human control).

And finally, under "perception of the self" they compare the manner in which people in different societies conceive of themselves (as separate individuals or as part of a tightly knit group) and how that affects the way they behave (emphasizing a reliance on self-motivation or acting in terms of obligation toward a group).

For the intercultural couple this means that there may be complex differences in their view of the world or vision of life behind many of the issues causing misunderstandings in their marriage, made all the more complex because those values are obscure. Most spouses don't know much about their own cultural value orientation (as they are just doing what comes naturally), much less that of their partner's.

---

[4] Stewart based his analysis on the Kluckhohn Model devised by Florence R. Kluckhohn and Fred L. Strodtbeck, in *Variations in Value Orientations* (Evanston, IL: Row and Peterson, 1961).

They just know when something isn't working right and automatically react defensively when their sense of "rightness" is attacked.

Dorrie, a Dutch woman (with an English mother) who married a Japanese man she met in graduate school in the United States (she was the student, he, the exalted professor), explained that it took her many years to begin to "spot the value differences which were at the bottom of most of our fights."

A seemingly trivial example explained what she meant. Like most Japanese, Dorrie and her husband, Hiroshi, slept on a futon, a Japanese-style mattress pad and quilts, which are hung out to air as often as possible. As Dorrie and Hiroshi lived in an apartment, that meant hanging them over the balcony, which she always did "with the side we sleep on facing out to get the most air and sun." Hiroshi regularly berated her for not hanging them so that the "pretty side" was out for others to see. He placed emphasis on appearance and was concerned about the impression they would make on neighbors, while she was more concerned about how much fresh air and sunlight the used side of the bedding would get. Behind this were two sets of cultural values, which in this case happened to conflict.

While this is a seemingly insignificant example of how value differences can cause disagreements, often couples move from minor issues to major ones, or from low gear into high. They begin talking about the two sides of a futon and escalate into slinging negative remarks at one another regarding the other's bad (different) upbringing, desire for control, or other irritation. Often couples never learn to identify what is actually behind the conflict. They never learn to recognize or empathize with the other's viewpoint or the history behind it. They think they are fighting about futons.

While we are all creatures of our cultural upbringing, not everyone adheres to the dominant values of his or her culture. Within each group are subgroups which may veer from, or actually oppose, the mainstream values. You will find intercultural spouses whose personal values do not coincide with the predominant cultural values of their society and who often identify more with aspects of those of their spouse's culture (which is possibly what attracted them to one another in the first place). Generally, people who enter into an intercultural marriage have already distanced themselves somewhat from a strict adherence to many of the predominant values of their own society. But, at the same time, their own culture's values are familiar territory for them, and to a certain degree they are what they are because of their society's value orientation. Whether they personally accept all of those values or not, they were shaped by a society which espoused them.

For example, although Jaime was a rebel who turned his back on his country, he was still a product of its values. He wanted to be free, like an American, to marry the girl of his choice without being restricted by social class, but his response to the menial job his choice forced him to accept was typically Latin American. He was outraged at the loss of dignity. Serving those he considered to be his inferiors clashed with his view of the way things were *supposed* to be; his background and social class demanded more. He was losing face, something which mattered to him, and he resented it.

Cassie, on the other hand, saw his job as a temporary expedient. To her it was a means to an end, and she couldn't understand why he was making such a big fuss about it. Although she was attracted to him for his very Latin personality, she wanted him to behave like a practical (American) man when necessity demanded it.

Deirdre is another spouse who was attracted to her partner's culture because it espoused many of the values she personally identified with, which were different from the dominant ones of her upbringing. Deirdre was an Irish woman, who at an early age had emigrated to the United States and was raised by energetic Irish-American Catholic relatives. She described herself as more of a "be-er" than a "do-er" and felt out of step with the society around her. She was more at home with others like her who wanted the world to slow down and allow her to smell the daisies rather than expecting her to conquer cyberspace. She always seemed to get along better with Latins and Hispanics, who, she felt, were more interested in interpersonal relationships and in having a good time than their Anglo-Saxon counterparts. When she met Mario, she was so taken with his playboy charm she didn't see that the man beneath was in many ways atypical of the Italian culture and was much more concerned with worldly achievement than spirituality and relationships.

Ironically, this is not an unusual occurrence in intercultural marriage—the partners in some important respect may identify more with the culture of the person they married than with their own and be blinded by their cultural stereotypes, not seeing the individual person beneath the surface.

At the other end of the spectrum are couples from cultures so widely divergent in the way right and wrong and good and bad are perceived that it is impossible for those who strictly adhere to their cultural tenets to coexist peaceably under the same roof. The key word here is *strictly*.

Yvette and Ali, the French-Kuwaiti couple we met at the beginning of the book, were about as culturally different as two people could be. Yvette, a baptized (although not churchgoing) Catholic, could not share many of Ali's values as dictated by his Islamic religion, especially in regard to male and female roles. Fortunately for them as a couple, Ali personally believed that each person should interpret the word of Allah in his or her own way and live accordingly, and he defended his wife against criticism from stricter Muslims. He believed that women should be more emancipated and, in fact, married a woman who could be more of an equal partner in the marriage than the traditional women of his own culture. But this tolerance, and the understanding based on it, had to be worked at continually in their daily lives, especially when they had children, who had to be taught right from wrong and proper behavior, which their parents didn't always define in the same way.

Similarity in values can help couples overcome differences in age, race, ethnicity, and religion. One American woman, describing her marriage to a Nigerian who was different from her in all of these respects, says that because they shared the same fundamental values, they had a happy marriage.

However, when conflicting values outweigh similarities, both spouses have to be ready to talk about and explore the meaning and depth of these differences, which is an especially difficult task for people from cultures that put little value on words for communication, but important for those from more verbal cultures. With honest, controlled, mutually respectful, and timely communication—not waiting until they are in the middle of a fight to unveil their feelings—each can learn to work at identifying where different and possibly contrasting values are at work. In most cases sorting this out is a lifetime task, but with practice it usually gets easier as couples become more skilled at it.

When the couple's conflicting values are deeply ingrained or completely unconscious, or when one or both of the partners is inflexible (will not admit to the existence of another value system), the marriage will be threatened. For it is only by understanding and being able to allow for one another's uniqueness, even regarding deeply held convictions about how life should be lived, that a married couple can continue to live in harmony.

4

Food and Drink

What is food to one is another's bitter poison.
—Lucretius, *On the Nature of Things*

Some wise person once said that compatibility in intercultural marriage has as much to do with garlic as with values.

In nearly all cultures food is used to celebrate or ritualize life events—to mark births, deaths, weddings. It is the main part of many ceremonies and rituals, both lay and religious, but it is also a mainstay of daily life. Food is what keeps body and soul together and, as such, can be one of the stickiest of the cultural issues.

Cookbooks from around the world show the diversity of taste, ingredients, and methods of preparing food. Etiquette books point out table manners and culinary protocol. Food brings out the characteristics of a people in many other ways: it shows something of the male-female relationship and roles, of the importance of family and religion, and of the lifestyle and values of a people.

Arabs enforce unity around the dinner table; the Irish drink at wakes,[1] the Japanese express Zen aesthetics through ritual tea ceremonies, and the stereotypical Jewish son shows love for his mother in proportion to his appetite. In Italy a woman's femininity has traditionally been judged according to how much time she spends bend-

---

[1] In Anglo-Irish families food is almost always less important than drink as an essential for ritual and celebration, and their lack of culinary prowess is an indication of the secondary importance they place on eating.

ing over the stove or kneading dough for the pasta. In certain Middle Eastern, Asian, and African countries, the men eat alone and the women cook, or supervise the cooking, and eat later. In others, where the women must not go out alone, the husband buys the food and the women prepare the meal with what he chooses. In Tunisia, where mealtimes are flexible and punctuality not important, the foods are such that they can be prepared ahead and reheated. In Morocco large divans surround tables which are always open to the unexpected guest, who may not only arrive unannounced but also stay for the night. In America frozen dinners are popped into the oven or microwave, freeing the cook and demonstrating the fast-paced, fragmented lifestyle of Americans.

Vive la difference!—until people from different cultural backgrounds live in the same house and deal with differences three times a day. In fact, no other single cultural difference was cited so often by couples as a problem as food. The significance goes far beyond the digestive tract. The intercultural couple has to work out house rules which satisfy them both, not only in terms of what is served but also how it is prepared and served and by whom, and who cleans up. These seemingly minor issues often become bones of contention between the spouses precisely because they contain so many underlying meanings and spring from so many unconscious sources.

Basically we can say that the food issue includes the following categories:

1. What is eaten (and drunk), how much of it, and how it is prepared

2. When the main meal is served—at noon or in the evening

3. Where the meal is eaten: in public or in private, in the car, on the street, on a mat on the floor or in the kitchen on the run; with or without the spouse and/or the children and with or without a paterfamilias at the head of a formal dinner table

4. How it is eaten (manners, utensils, etc.)

What Is Eaten

Fish and chips...sushi......*fejoiada*...*matouke*...peanut butter... curry...lasagna...wonton...blood sausage...sea slugs...stuffed vine leaves...and so on; the list is endless, and each food is a mainstay to someone.

Religious taboos and special customs enter in: Muslim law prohibits the consumption of alcoholic beverages, pork, and shellfish; Hindus avoid beef, and Buddhists, all flesh; Catholics fast on Good Friday; Jews observe Passover; and Muslims fast from dawn until dusk during Ramadan.

Some people are open to experimentation while others are tied psychologically to certain tastes. Still others may not be able to digest the ethnic fare of the partner or may even be allergic to it.

One Swedish husband, Sune, complained that the smell of his wife, Rani's, Malaysian cooking nauseated him. A Scottish bride never could get used to her Iranian husband's "raw onion breath."[2] Victor, who was used to homogenized Swiss fare, had to swallow his horror (and more) when his Tunisian mother-in-law honored him with the choice morsel at their first dinner together: the bubbling eye which stared out at him from the skewered sheep's head roasting over the hearth.

More often the couple's food problems are subtle ones, based on what each one is used to and prefers in his or her home: a meal is not a meal without borscht, without rice, without fresh bread, without wine, without meat and potatoes, and so on.

Longing for one's own foods may play a powerful psychological role in marriage, especially in the lives of spouses who have left their homelands to live in their partner's country. The American may wish for a hamburger and fries to soothe a bout of homesickness; the British, a traditional pudding at Christmas; the Vietnamese, a meal of rice and ginger chicken shared with friends and relatives.

Occasionally the disdain one partner feels for the food (or the manner of preparing or eating it) of the other becomes a silent re-

---

[2] Almost everyone tends to prefer the smells one grew up with and which ring the bells of childhood memories; some never accept alien aromas.

proach. Chilean Miguel chided his American wife, Carol, and her compatriots for what he saw as their excessive consumption of beer and
other alcoholic beverages. Sometimes the spouse's inability to dupli-
cate the fare of the other is a cause for criticism or brings on feelings
of inadequacy in the cook. One American woman commented that
she was the brunt of her husband's jokes to his French friends because "I didn't know how to pinch the Brie and therefore was considered incompetent and incapable of doing the shopping alone." Another, married to an Italian, remembers a Christmas being ruined because she had put tomatoes into (had ruined) the broth for the traditional *tortellini in brodo*. A Palestinian husband recalls his Mexican
wife's anger when he refused to taste an elaborate Mexican dinner
she had prepared for him. "She was so mad she sat down right in
front of me and ate the entire meal for two. She nearly made herself
sick, and I went without dinner that night."

"The way to a man's heart is through his stomach" goes the old
adage, and usually the stomach wants the kind of food it is used to.
Love is shown in a lot of ways, but in many cultures love and caring
are judged by the time and effort put into preparing the repast. In
others, food preparation is much less significant as an indicator of
love and devotion. The important thing is to understand and empathize with the partner's feelings about it.

Yvette, who had met her Kuwaiti husband when both were students in England, resented it when he called her from her studies to
bring him a cup of tea, something he could easily have done for himself. He was puzzled by her view of this simple ritual as a sexist demand. Later she learned to accept such requests as his way of using
a food ritual to call her attention to him, of asking her to demonstrate
her love for him.

When the Meal Is Served

Sara, a flight attendant for Air Canada, had lived alone and had her
free time to herself before she married Joachim, an established Portuguese industrialist fifteen years her senior. When he was working,
she thought she would be free to spend her days as she chose. He
saw things differently, however, and their controversy over the noon

meal was their earliest and most continuous battle. She maintained that she had promised "for better, for worse, but never for lunch." Joachim expected an elaborate noon feast, and she found that her whole life was scheduled around this intrusive constant: shopping for lunch, preparing it, eating it, and cleaning up after it. Her days were no longer free and she became increasingly resentful. He was offended by her neglectful attitude toward her wifely role and reproached her for her inability to conform gracefully to the customs of his country, where everything shut down for two hours in the middle of the day and all married men went home for the main meal and a rest.

For many intercultural couples mealtime is an issue. Some of them cannot accustom their stomachs to new schedules: one may simply not be hungry at noon or the other may not be able to eat a big meal at night. Some want to eat at the same time every day, while others prefer to eat when they are hungry. Much depends on the degree of formality in the family they grew up in, which often depends on where the family is from.

Where the Meal Is Eaten

Where a family chooses to eat its main meal varies also and tells a great deal about whether the family is formal or informal, united or fragmented, authoritarian or permissive.

For Sara and Joachim, the noon meal was a cause of disagreement, not only in regard to what and when but to where as well. For him a meal was not to be snapped up while perched on a stool in the kitchen. It was a formal affair in which the entire family met around the table in the dining room, which was set with a tablecloth and silver...every day, not just on Sunday. When the children were old enough to join them, the noon meal became a time of instruction on etiquette as well: how to sit, chew, be served, and use utensils (a problem since he and Sara held their forks in opposite hands). In the best of moments it was a time to be together, to share what was going on in their lives; in the worst (to Sara) it was a time of tempers, torture, and bad digestion.

How the Meal Is Eaten

How the meal is eaten also depends on the customs and manners of each partner's culture. Sara and Joachim held their forks in different hands, Cecil used a fork and knife, and Ikumi, chopsticks. Stefan used monogrammed utensils and linens; and Cristina had grown up mostly with finger food.

Other couples have to decide how the table is to be set (if it is to be set), who sits and who serves, and what constitutes good or bad manners according to their own family practices. In some cultures, it is appropriate to slurp soup or burp to indicate appreciation of the meal, while in others such behavior raises eyebrows, at the least.

Joachim considered it ill-mannered to eat fruit at the table with one's hands, and Sara was ineffective in peeling and slicing oranges with a knife and fork. For the first months of their marriage she ate only grapes, which didn't have to be peeled (but longed for the seedless ones from home). She thought paper napkins made sense with small children, but they were repugnant to Joachim.

These small things can be daily irritants; often one partner is disdainful of the other's "bad" manners. One partner may resent being pressured to conform to unfamiliar customs, while the other complains because the partner hasn't managed to adapt well. When there are also children, the couple may argue continually about the whole matter, creating a tug-of-war at mealtime.

For many couples, however, the differences in food tastes and customs are a source of humor more than discord. Food stories are the ones they most love to tell on one another. One Japanese husband married to an American described the crisis he faced every Thanksgiving when he had to be the "man of the house" and carve the traditional turkey. "I usually hacked the poor bird to shreds." He also looked on the cranberry sauce as his dessert, something the whole family eventually imitated and created a "cranberry pie," thus transforming this one-culture celebration into a bicultural one.

5

Sex

> Amoebas at the start
> Were not complex
> They tore themselves apart
> And started Sex.

—Arthur Guiterman

It has been said that in every sexual relationship a couple takes four sets of grandparents to bed with them. What this means is that each partner is the product of sex education passed down from what the grandparents taught the parents, and each brings a version of (or reaction to) their mores, credos, and expectations into his or her own marriage—whether consciously or not.

In any case, this is a startling image, and if we think of it in terms of intercultural marriage, with the vast range of possible different beliefs, behaviors, and attitudes vying for position under one blanket, we see why sex can become a real issue.

Simply listing some of the things which can be viewed differently by people from various cultures gives some idea of how far-reaching the issue of sex might be in these marriages:

> arranged marriage, abortion, contraception, infertility, menstruation, female mutilation, circumcision, masturbation, sex education, the number (and importance) of children in a family, virginity and chastity, family honor, adolescent rites, machismo and femininity, homosexuality, hygiene, premarital relations, sexual practices, prostitution, incest, dating, dancing, romance, holding hands, using makeup, and "provocative" dress.

One reason sex can be a problem in intercultural marriage is that many, especially young, inexperienced people, don't expect it to be. Sex and communication are said to be two of the least problematic *premarital* issues in monocultural as well as bicultural relationships. But even fairly sophisticated people, who feel freer to discuss sex openly, often give out contradictory messages about the power and the pleasure as well as sometimes the shame they associate with sexuality. Many people are prepared for differences in ways of eating, dressing, or talking, but they assume that sex is sex—which, of course, it is, with infinite variety in its expression. So perhaps out of primness, embarrassment, or reticence of any kind, they don't find out beforehand about possible differences in beliefs, behaviors, and expectations that will affect them *once they are married*. Often they don't openly discuss their needs and wants—and have perhaps not truly even defined them.

Couples who have lived together before marriage have some practical advantages, but they can also be in for surprises when marriage changes the format of their relationship as independent lovers and each begins to play the role (as each one sees it) of husband or wife.

Yvette, for example, commented that Ali, who had been attentive to her needs and affectionate in his lovemaking when they were living together, not only stopped being so once they were married but was actually disconcerted by her need for cuddling and kissing. He was, as he said, put off by her demands for sexual satisfaction and felt that her forward behavior was inappropriate, if not improper, for a wife.

American Rashida discovered many years after they were married that, although her Kenyan husband, Olu, had willingly participated in premarital sex with her, the fact that she had permitted it caused him to distrust her for the rest of their married life. He felt that if she had slept with him, she was capable of "sinning" in that way in the future. The fact that she told him he was the only one did not pacify him, and any action of hers which he could interpret as provocative, he saw as a sign of her wantonness. To her dismay, he even considered her style of dress, use of makeup, and friendship with single male friends inappropriate for a married woman.

Dutch Protestant Dorrie, on the other hand, was upset by what she called "the gymnastic, uninhibited sex" her Japanese husband preferred and which she found somewhat shocking and unsatisfying. "It is all so cut and dried," she commented, "technically perfect but lacking in the displays of affection I need. Where is the wine, the romance?"

Couples with the same religious background have an advantage in that they know what the moral dictates of the religion are and can agree (to some extent) on what is and is not permitted (or required) in sexual matters. But as Irish-Catholic Deirdre discovered with her wandering Italian-Catholic husband, the same religion does not always mean similar moral education, because that religion is often interpreted in different ways cross-culturally. Sins may be sins, but in certain cultures they are mortal and in others venal. The difference is the degree of guilt associated with the sin. In certain male-dominant cultures, the double standard is more pronounced; what is sinful for women is overlooked in men.

Much depends on how differing cultures view the meaning of marriage, the role of romantic love, and the position women hold in general (and thus in the marital relationship).

The position of women under the law will affect sexual practices in the marriage. Dr. Hakima Himmich, president of the Moroccan Association to Fight AIDS, reports that the dramatic increase of AIDS in northern Africa is partly due to the inability (for fear of being divorced) of wives either to refuse sex or to insist that their husbands use condoms—even when both know of the husband's infidelity.[1] In some fundamentalist countries foreign (Christian, Jewish, Hindi) women are subject to strict Islamic laws.

In a marriage in which traditionally the woman belongs to or is the server of her husband and the man the master, the woman's pleasure will be of little importance—certainly second to the man's.

Although Rashida and Olu's marriage was one of true love, he believed that women exist to serve men, that marriage means family, and that procreation is the main purpose of sex, that is, having children certifies the validity of the marriage. Rashida was pressured, not

---

[1] Dr. Hakima Himmich, head of the Moroccan Association to Fight AIDS, during a talk at the FAWCO Conference in Casablanca, March 1993.

only by Olu but by his entire family, to begin a family immediately (with the ever-present unspoken threat of his possibly taking a second wife if she didn't).[2]

In societies where marriage is seen primarily as a romantic union of two people (most frequently egalitarian societies), the pleasure and needs of the two partners (physical, psychological, and social) will be important. Sex, although important, may take second place to other things; and when the marriage is between equals, the sexual life of the couple will follow patterns of give and take and mutual pleasure in giving and seeking. Massimo and Tove, who were best friends as well as lovers, found that while at first it was necessary to learn about and respect each other's personal proclivities, their confident delight in one another grew over the years and served as a way to smooth over other disagreements and problems.

Even for couples from societies which share the belief that romantic love is an important ingredient for marriage, there may be quite different ways of expressing that love, that is, how sex is used to give or deny love, how lustily it is enjoyed, or how openly and honestly it is discussed. Deirdre, for example, could never quite shake loose many of her Irish-Catholic ingrained inhibitions and beliefs that some sexual practices were sinful, although she thought she had put these ideas far behind her when she married Mario. He felt she had not been totally honest about how she felt; she had not known how to confront delicate feelings. No one in her family had taught her to speak openly and honestly about "such things."

Some couples only have problems when they become parents, when the roles of mother/father are added to those of husband/wife. From the moment pregnancy is confirmed, there is often a change on the part of one or the other partner in his or her attitude or treatment of the other, which is reflected in their sexual practices. New mothers may not want to be or may not be considered appropriate sexual

---

2   Imamura, in "Husband–Wife Role Misunderstanding," explores the sources of role dissensus in marriage, using data from foreign women married to Nigerians. In this article she quotes one wife who says, "Even though the wife has children, there is pressure to have sons.... I have to admit, when I had that boy, the whole neighborhood knew.... I screamed and yelled...it's a boy! it's a boy! And it's only one reason that I could be so excited, and that is that I had fulfilled my obligation."

partners for a certain period of time after giving birth. Both partners may not see this the same way and may feel frustrated or rejected by the other.

When the couple become parents, many old mores and taboos, which may have been abandoned or compromised in the enthusiasm of romance, often return to the foreground. Then the real challenge begins. For when there are children to educate, each parent reverts, often unconsciously, to what he or she was taught during childhood, so as to pass along the right moral code to the children.

Jaime, the student from Santo Domingo who was originally attracted to Cassie because of her free ways, criticized her for those very ways when it came time to inculcate a moral code in their daughter Jennifer. What was all right for him and Cassie was wrong when it came to educating Jennifer. Though the world in which Jennifer was growing up was much more permissive than Jaime and Cassie's, Jaime took two steps backward into the culture he had supposedly left behind.

Olu frequently threatened Rashida that he was going to take their boys away from her and send them to his mother to be educated in the "proper" way. Because many of her beliefs and practices were different from his, he said she was not a fit mother. Their sons' sexual (as well as intellectual) education was a source of constant conflict between them.

Swiss Victor was amazed when his wife, Zehyra, who he thought had become sophisticated and worldly in her years and miles away from her homeland, began imparting her Tunisian mores and customs to their adolescent daughter. He especially disagreed with her insistence that the girl shave her entire body in order to be considered clean and attractive.

The free-spirited Rio de Janeiroan Carioca, Maria Clotilde, did not want her son to undergo the formal ceremony of circumcision (which was part of Zoahar's Israeli culture), in which guests were invited and a professional circumciser hired for the occasion. It was alien to her; this was *her* baby too; he was not entirely Israeli, and her upbringing caused her to feel that the ceremony was barbaric. Finally, however, she realized how important it was to Zoahar and reluctantly agreed to it.

Many couples manage to work out their culturally based sexual differences with few problems because of their own ethnosensitivity and open communication. It helps, of course, if they happen to be of the same social and educational backgrounds, the same generation and religion, and with basically the same moral values, even if different cultures. Many believe that sex should be the least of their cultural problems, but often just the opposite is true. Much depends on just how culturally different the two people are, how grounded they are in their culture or religious dictates regarding sex, how much importance they themselves attach to sex in their relationship, and how openly and honestly they can communicate about it and work to resolve conflict.

6

Male-Female Roles

> Marriage *n.* The state or condition of a community con-
> sisting of a master, a mistress and two slaves, making in all,
> two.
>
> —Ambrose Bierce, *The Devil's Dictionary*

In even the most progressive societies, true equality between the sexes is more a goal than a reality. As pointed out by John C. Condon and Fathi Yousef, it is the *form* of male superiority which differs from culture to culture. In some societies, primarily non-Western ones, "...the woman's role is to serve the man—including, often, doing hard physical labor, deferring to his judgments, and socially subordinating herself in such ways as walking behind him and eating after he has eaten."[1]

In Western societies, on the other hand, male dominance takes a more subtle form: the woman is afforded certain courtesies (which designate her as the weaker sex), and certain customs are followed that demonstrate the man's authority. These have traditionally been indicated by who holds the door, pays the restaurant check, buys the house, or takes the other's name in marriage. In fact it is many of these customs that have been targeted with some success by feminists in their battle for equality (and defended by women who are happy with the status quo). "In either case there are many activities that are limited to men and others that are the exclusive province of

---

[1] John C. Condon and Fathi Yousef, *An Introduction to Intercultural Communication* (New York: Macmillan, 1975), 70.

women, but *the specific activities vary considerably from culture to culture* (author's italics).[2]

So important is this issue in marital compatibility that spouses who view their respective gender roles in the same basic way often find that most of their other cultural differences will fall into place without too much difficulty. For example, Bill (from the United States) and Mary (from Nigeria) as well as Eva (from Germany) and Duncan (from the United States) had in common with their spouses their belief that while the husband's main responsibility was outside the home, the wife ran the home without interference. But in both cases, the women also had satisfactory activities and jobs outside, and the men participated (to some degree) within. They had the same ideas about what partnership in marriage meant.

However, when two people from cultures which view these roles differently marry and attempt to build a familial structure, the differences may become a major issue. This is especially true if (1) the societies are culturally far apart, (2) one or both of the spouses adheres strictly to his or her society's interpretation of gender roles, (3) the man comes from a male-dominant culture and the woman from an egalitarian one, and (4) the couple lives in the country with the stricter male-female role delineation (especially if the woman is the foreigner).

If one of the partners is forced to adhere to a severely different role delineation from the one that was customary at home, there may be problems, and the wider the gap between the partners' cultures, the more severe those problems may be.

One young woman from Iceland, a country where women enjoy equal rights and responsibilities with men (and where a woman, Vigdis Finnbogadottir, was elected president), suffered a significant loss of personal freedom and recognition when she married a man from Saudi Arabia. She was at first incredulous, then outraged, to discover the extent to which in some parts of today's world women are still denied their rights and independence, are cloistered from men, and are expected to wear the veil and black *abaya* in public. It was small consolation to her when her husband tried to explain to her that the

---

[2] Ibid., 70–71.

women really had a lot of power: "In this culture it is the women who make all the decisions but the men *say* the decisions." She also resented the fact that he had not been completely honest with her regarding what her life was going to be like once they moved to Riyadh from France, where they had both been living (she had been unable to visit before they were married).

Dorrie, on the other hand, commented that one of her greatest difficulties, especially at first, was accepting the fact that she was expected to handle not only the family budget by herself without any help from her husband, but also the children. "It took me some time to learn just what the Japanese maxim of 'a good husband is healthy and…absent' meant in terms of spheres of action. Here I'm on my own in these responsibilities."

Milee also suffered from what she called too much liberty when she left the protected lifestyle of her home in Saigon for the wide open spaces of Australia, where she was "thrust out on [her] own," forced to learn to drive a car (which terrified her), and spend nights alone when her journalist husband was away on assignment. She was not accustomed to going out and around by herself and to making major decisions and purchases, and her poor knowledge of English intensified her fearfulness. The Australian women she met assumed that she was delighted with her improved female status, but Milee felt betrayed and neglected, was ashamed of her husband who, she felt, didn't really care about her and didn't know the "manly" way to take care of and protect his wife.

Harry, Milee's husband, was bewildered and annoyed by the helplessness of his timorous wife. He felt that she was dumping total responsibility for her life and happiness on him and not pulling her own weight. Why couldn't she recognize that he was treating her with respect by giving her a say in the major decisions and duties? He began to feel suffocated by her inability to adjust to Australian ways, by her clinging attachment to him, and by the totality of his responsibility. He needed a wife who was a partner and found himself with one who was a "stone around his neck."

Jaime also struggled with the battle between his personal beliefs regarding men's and women's roles and those which were the rule in the United States. When Cassie had to find a part-time job to help them meet expenses (leaving him at home to care for Jennifer), he had a "hard time holding [his] head up." He was humiliated to be left with what in Santo Domingo would be considered women's work, with not being able to provide for his family, and with having to depend on her salary to augment his insufficient income. It was worse when he had to turn to her for help in preparing their income tax forms, which he could not decipher, or in translating his accented English to public officials. Worse still, he felt she was beginning to want to "wear the pants in the family" when she argued that she had as much right as he to decide what they were going to do with their combined salaries.

All of these spouses had expected their partners to be foreign reflections of their own preconceived notions of what a husband or wife should be. They had expected differences, even looked forward to them, but not in the basic role function. They felt betrayed by their spouses; instead, they had really been betrayed by their different understanding of their respective roles. For example, Milee expected Harry to be her savior. She did not expect him to "push her in and let her swim," and so she was disillusioned and disappointed. He never dreamed that she wouldn't "shape up and take on her own share of the load" after she had adjusted to his country. He felt tricked by fate.

Of course, many partners are well traveled and expect their spouse's culture to be different. Furthermore, not every person adheres to his or her own culture's beliefs and behaviors. Many also do not like the way their own society has assigned gender roles. Some women might want to escape the responsibilities of their own culture and be willing to sacrifice some of their freedom in exchange for being taken care of. Some might prefer a culture in which the role of wife and mother is glorified and clear-cut in regard to duties and rights.

Daniele, a Belgian woman married to a Western-educated and upper-class Moroccan and living in the cosmopolitan city of Casablanca, said that she reveled in the benefits of being in the wife-mother honored position, while retaining freedom from the more stringent dictates of Islamic womanhood. "I never have to cook, clean, or do the wash," she explained. "I have a driver and a dressmaker and have more free time to do the things I like than I would have in Belgium. I don't envy my women friends in Belgium who are trying to juggle full responsibility for home and children with demanding and competitive careers in which they may succeed or fail. I'm in a no-lose position. I admit that it's a bit of a gilded cage syndrome in many ways, but the lifestyle suits me just fine."

What's important is being in *agreement* about the roles, not in how they are actually divided.[3] However, it can usually be said that when the man is from a male-dominant culture and the woman from an egalitarian one, the problem is going to be harder to resolve than the other way around. Women, irrespective of culture, tend to be more relationship-oriented than men and to give more to keep the relationship going, but with a man who considers that the woman's role is to serve him or who considers her inferior, she has to give much more—and has to give *up* much more.

Foreign wives often lament that they cannot find stimulating or enriching jobs in their husband's country or jobs which are at the level of the ones they had back home, either because of labor laws, their lack of proficiency in the language, or prejudice against working wives or mothers. Others struggle alone to balance home and work, often in barely satisfactory jobs, and sometimes subjecting themselves to the disapproval of husband and/or society in order to maintain some degree of independence and a sense of their own identity in the foreign land.[4]

For Toronto-born Sara, it wasn't so much the two hours a day revolving around Joachim's lunch which bothered her as it was the fact that it, not she, was organizing her life. She was constantly "on call" to his wishes. She felt as though what she wanted didn't count anymore, that she was valued only insofar as she adhered to his interpretation of what a good wife does. In many ways she longed for the days when she had had a career that gave her some independent identity, and she was very supportive of younger foreign wives she met who were struggling to keep up both career and marriage, often against the wishes of their husbands.

---

[3] Being in agreement may have as much to do with being of the same social status as anything else. More on this in chapter 13.

[4] However, in many non-Western and developing countries, educated Western women actually do quite well finding positions which are at least equal to those they would find at home.

Cassie, though living in her own country, often felt that upon marrying Jaime she had emigrated to a foreign land. On the one hand, she complained that she was being treated like a subordinate, having to fight for her God-given (American) rights to see whom she wanted, where and when, and to spend her own money as she saw fit. On the other hand, she had to handle many things men in her culture usually took care of because her foreign husband was unable to do so. Jaime was faced with the complicated problem of remaining manly in his own eyes as well as those of both his wife and the society around him.

Both Cassie and Sara resented the unfamiliar and unexpected restraints on their accustomed freedom; both men were upset and surprised that their wives were so unwilling to perform their role as wives in a truly "womanly" way and felt their masculinity was threatened.

Where the couple lives often tempers their interpretation of their roles as men and women: whether they live in urban or rural settings, where role delineations may be more strictly adhered to; and whether they are in the husband's, the wife's, or a third country. When Yvette and Ali lived as fellow students in London, their relationship was that of friends as well as lovers. Each did his or her own share of work in the flat; each respected the other's dedication to earning a degree; and each helped and encouraged the other toward that end.

But when they moved back to Kuwait, where male and female roles are clearly defined and adhered to, Ali felt obligated to dominate his foreign wife when his family and friends were around and to make her conform to the role of wife as it was seen in his culture. Yvette bristled under the unaccustomed bridle but was wise enough to defer to him in public so that he would not lose face. She made it quite clear, however, that she was not going to become a Kuwaiti wife in the privacy of their own home. It was not easy. Ali constantly received subtle pressures from his culture and unconsciously fell back into his old ways and viewpoints. He felt torn between what he had been raised to expect and what his wife wanted. It was also hard for Yvette to keep up the battle. But, as she said, it was easier to "keep on fighting" than to "face the fatigue of trying to live up to ideals and according to values not shared." She felt that it was essential for the longevity of the relationship that she maintain her independence to some degree.

Anne Imamura relates how foreign wives (living in Nigeria) must adjust to the expectations and behavior not only of their husbands but of their husband's kin. "They [have to] learn to take from kin criticisms of their deviance from the norms of appropriate womanly behavior" and realize "that they gain local acceptance to the extent that they conform to local practices."[5]

In other cultures, however, some Western women relate that the women of the country often encourage them to deviate from the local customs in order to make a statement about female emancipation. Daniele said that any overt compliance on her part to domineering treatment by her husband was considered a betrayal by her educated Moroccan women friends. They liked to use her more egalitarian marriage as an example to hold up to their own husbands. Her best ally of them all, however, was her sister-in-law Hafsa, who had married an American and become an outspoken advocate of women's rights.

Sometimes cultures seem more similar than they really are and so the couples are truly unprepared for the subtle differences, especially in role definition. Some unexpectedly difficult combinations are those between English and Americans, Danes and Swedes, Filipinos and Indonesians, and Japanese and Koreans, because these cultures, which appear similar on the surface, are really much more diverse than either partner imagines.

Italian Mario and his Irish wife, Deirdre, although of two Western, not widely divergent cultures, never saw eye-to-eye regarding the duties, domain, and privileges of husband and wife and thus were never able to live up to each other's expectations. Mario wanted and expected a wife who gave him her constant and unquestioning moral support and respect simply because he fulfilled his obligations as successful wage earner and strong father. Deirdre believed that respect was not automatic but had to be earned, and she was not good at hiding her feelings about this. Instead of agreeing with things she felt were wrong, she challenged him. Instead of complying, she fought back; she never managed the *dolce fregolotta* (or "catch more flies

---

[5] Anne E. Imamura, "The Loss That Has No Name," *Gender and Society* 2, no. 3 (September 1988): 291–307.

with honey") approach, typical of his countrywomen, to achieve her ends.

He complained that she did not know how to be sweet and feminine or how to be a real wife, claiming that she wanted "a sparring partner instead of a husband." In fact, that was partially true, but Deirdre also wanted someone who enjoyed her company, shared her interests, and supported her in her search for self-growth, which, according to Mario, was "feminist drivel." Because of their cultural biases, neither was able to comprehend fully, agree with, or satisfy the other's vision of what a husband or wife should be.

Obviously, theirs was a personal as well as a cultural impasse based as much on stubborn inflexibility as cultural socialization, but there is no doubt that their personal expectations of marriage and their roles as husband and wife, man and woman within that marriage were culturally infused. Each considered the other's way to be wrong. Both clung to what their own cultures taught, and they fought over the details.

The male-female role issue is tied up with subtle and often intangible ideas regarding the meaning of marriage and intimacy; the necessity of respect, integrity, and mutual support; and questions of power. These are the underlying issues which are often not discussed but must be sorted out. If they are not, both spouses (whose expectations have not been understood and met) can feel betrayed, misunderstood, cheated, or rejected; and, ultimately, either or both may feel like a failure for not being able to live up to the other's ideals.

7

Time

Time is the most valuable thing a man can spend.
—Theophrastus, "Diogenes Laërtius"
Lives of Eminent Philosophers

When it is past in Paris, it is present in New York and future in Hong Kong...that is, if you are in New York.

We all know that there are different times all over the world. Anyone who has traveled over time zones has experienced jet lag—when one's body is not on the same time as the clock on the street corner. Many are vaguely aware that in different parts of the world the concept, that is, the meaning and value of time, varies.

The question "How late is late?" is not answered the same way from culture to culture, nor is the notion of being on time assigned equal importance. Some countries (the United States, for instance) are concerned with punctuality, with saving time, because they are countries based on future growth, and every moment counts toward building that future. Other countries (Latin American or Arab, for example) place more importance on *using* time than being on time; they believe in making the most of each moment by fully living it, because as a rule they are more interested in the quality of present life than in the future.

Although no culture is purely present-, past-, or future-oriented, the importance each places on temporal frames of reference varies, and, as a result, people in different parts of the world move at different paces. In Latin American and Arab countries they are generally more relaxed and unhurried, engaging in time-consuming courtesies and conversations. To them, interpersonal activities are more important than meeting the demands of an external timekeeper. On the other hand, in the United States the emphasis is on productivity; time must be managed efficiently. People are in a hurry, often overlooking the interpersonal aspects of life.

Tomorrow means specifically the day after today in English but becomes *mañana* in Spanish and *bukra* in Arabic, both of which refer to a less defined time in the future.

Anthropologist Edward T. Hall, in his studies on the cultural nature of time, has found that different cultures move to various rhythmic patterns, and so do individuals. Individual rhythm is inherent, that is, it "begins in the center of the self." Each person has his or her own sense of time and of pace and lives accordingly. But each individual has also been trained to conform to certain cultural rhythms from the moment of birth. Each culture has been "choreographed in its own way, with its own beat, tempo and rhythm." Thus, "while personality is undoubtedly a factor in interpersonal synchrony, culture is also a powerful determinant." Though not every individual is in sync with his or her own culture, people generally gauge themselves according to a central time clock.[1]

Frequently, people who marry outside their cultural group are incompatible with their own culture and more attuned to the rhythms of another—often that of the spouse, which might partially account for the attraction between the two. For example, an American who marries a Japanese might be someone who, while admiring progress, deplores the American habit of continuously tearing down the old to make way for the new or its obsession with youth, and feels more attuned to a culture which venerates its elders and values its traditions more strongly.

But, generally speaking, intercultural spouses are products of their own culture's time clock, which is frequently different from that of their partner's. They may find that their dissimilar, unconscious rhythms

---

[1]   Edward T. Hall, *The Dance of Life* (New York: Anchor Books/Doubleday, 1983), 146, 163, 181.

and time patterns are being violated when they set up house together and react emotionally to situations.

When these couples first meet, they are usually aware of such differences, but as they fall in love, the differences are temporarily suspended and each feels at one with the other. Only later, in the settling-in phase, do they tend to return to their original rhythms and occasionally find that each is moving to a different drummer. Perhaps one is always late, or the other is always in a hurry, or one doesn't want to take the time for the little formal rituals which the other can't live without.

Hafsa's American husband, Mike, as an airline pilot, had to live with a schedule. He timed everything, including how long it took his Moroccan wife, Hafsa, to get to the point whenever she called someone on the phone. He prided himself on not wasting time and on knowing how to cut through the "senseless formalities" of the people around him. She had her hands full trying to explain to her friends that he was just "being American," not rude.

Occasionally, couples find that they are actually throwing each other off balance but don't know why. Many couples learn the other partner's rhythm and change their own, or they both adapt to the rhythm of the country where they live. But there is an inner time clock that does not change entirely, and if these inner clocks are too dissimilar, the partners may actually find they are "unnerved by the stranger in the house who moves to a different beat," as German Helga experienced with her Libyan husband.

> His time and my time are so different that more and more we find we are doing things separately to avoid bickering. He resents my harping at him and says I try to keep track of his movements. He won't wear a watch, says he doesn't need it. For him time is rubber, it stretches. But I go mad when he says he's going out for fifteen minutes and comes back three hours later without any explanation. I have no schedules to work my day around, can never count on him to be on time for anything—movies, parties, even dinner. He is never *ever* on time for dinner. He believes in eating when he is hungry!

Zoahar and Maria Clotilde (who met in the limbo-land of Club Med) explained their time-orientation problems in another way. "It affects the grand scheme of how we want to live our lives," says Zoahar.

> For example, she wanted me to stay on at Club Med, where time stands still (there is no growth potential), because it was fun, varied; we got to change destinations every six months. But I needed to begin to settle down, perhaps start a family, plan for the future, have the security a solid bank account can provide. She calls me stingy, uptight, says she doesn't care about the future—she'll be old then. She wants to have fun now. She quotes Octavio Paz to me: 'Whoever builds a house for future happiness, builds a prison for the present.'

Joachim and Sara acknowledge that their lunch feud is based as much on differing ideas of time as anything else. It isn't only that he resents Sara's not wanting to take the time to prepare his meal, he physically misses the break in the middle of the day—his body rebels. While Sara resents the imposition and is secretly disdainful of a man who wastes hours at the lunch table and sleeps half the afternoon away, she also finds her body won't halt and relax in the middle of the day. Nonetheless, she has had to conform to the ways of the land, and as she moves more into middle age, it seems less difficult to slow down. Still she often finds herself "sitting on the edge of the chair, waiting for the eternal meal to end and pacing the floor waiting for everyone to wake up and get on with life."

As Sara found, the spouse who is living in the partner's country not only has to get in tune with his or her partner, but with the rhythms of the land as well. This definitely takes some extra adjustment, especially for the more mobile couples who move frequently to other countries during their married lives.

Although in time couples do adapt to one another's rhythm or learn philosophically to allow for it, still a spouse from one culture can be slowed down only so much and a spouse from the other speeded up just so much before the strain shows.

8

Place of Residence

Now you're with the man you've always wanted. In a place
you don't belong.
                    —Robbie Clipper Sethi, *The Bride Wore Red*

By the very nature of our definition of the union, one partner in an
intercultural marriage is the foreigner and has to learn to live and
function in a foreign country, unless they live in a third country. This
spouse, despite how much affinity he or she may have for the new
land (or lack of attachment to the homeland), will experience a degree
of homesickness, that is, loss of home and the security of a fully com-
prehended ambiance. A sense of unresolved sadness over this loss
can exist in an otherwise very happy marriage. Eva, for example, confessed that although she has adjusted to living in the United States
since Duncan retired from the Foreign Service, she doesn't really like
it and feels the necessity of going back to Europe regularly for "my
cultural fix.... Some things you adjust to right away," she explains.
"Some, never."

The country where the couple lives, the degree to which the culture is similar to that of the expatriate spouse, and the couple's loca-
tion (urban or rural) will all affect their relationship. Like it or not, the
world outside the door will intrude on their marriage, be it his land,
her land, or a neutral third one. Regardless of their individual cultures
or the style they have chosen for their marriage, they will have deal-
ings with the people of their chosen country and will have to respect
its customs and values. They will have to observe the laws of the land

and will be touched by the climate, the living conditions, the political situation, and the moral standards. They will also be affected by the way the society at large (family and neighbors as well as strangers) views their marriage.

Bill, who was originally from Texas, and his Nigerian wife, Mary, realized this very early in their relationship. Although their immediate families finally accepted their marriage, they often found themselves the objects of open or covert racism on the part of strangers. While they were in the university atmosphere, they had few problems of this nature because there were a number of interracial couples with whom they made friends. They always thought twice about traveling elsewhere, however. Going to visit Bill's parents in a rural Texas town, for instance, was problematic. How would Bill and Mary and their biracial children be treated? Would they be accepted? What unknowns were they going to encounter which might drive a wedge between them? The attitude of society toward their marriage was a constant concern, and although it had the effect of binding them closer to one another, it influenced many of the life decisions they made.

In some countries it is the difference in the religion of the two partners that will be the cause of societal disapproval and subject them to antagonism. In Northern Ireland, for example, a foreign same-faith marriage is seen with less animosity than a Catholic–Protestant one, because the latter is seen as an indication that the two people have "turned their backs not only on their religion, but also on the whole tradition within which they have been raised."[1]

In other countries the society may be indifferent toward the mixed marriage, especially if no children are born of the union. Still others welcome marriages between people from different lands. Often much depends on how physically similar the expatriate spouse is to the people of the country where the couple lives, how much he or she stands out. Dorrie, with her blond hair and blue eyes, complained of "people looking at me like I'm a freak" when she went out in Japan.

---

[1] Hastings Donnan, "Mixed Marriage in Comparative Perspective: Gender and Power in Northern Ireland and Pakistan," *Journal of Comparative Family Studies* 21, no. 2 (Summer 1990): 213.

Aside from the external effect of a country on a marriage, the marital pattern itself may be affected by the place of residence. The pattern that the couple adopted in one country and which worked for them there will not necessarily work in another. There may be a change in roles and/or of the balance of power within the relationship. Cultural traits which were perceived in one way in one country may be seen differently in another.

Wherever the intercultural couple goes, there is adapting to be done, and adapting means effort and sometimes strain. Problems which stem from where the couple is living differ according to the people and the circumstances:

1. Some couples meet in the country of one of the partners and remain there. Thus, one spouse is at home and the other is already familiar with the style of life in that country and already functions there more or less successfully.

2. Some meet in the country of one partner, then marry and move to the country of the other. Most frequently (but certainly not always) it is the bride who follows her husband to his homeland and has to learn and adapt to a whole new set of living patterns in order to function and be accepted in that country.

3. Others meet and remain in or move to a country which is home to neither of them. Thus both are expatriates, with the job not only of working out a marital style which incorporates their two cultures, but of adapting personally and as a couple to a third style. There are many couples who maintain that living in a third country is the only (or ideal) way for an intercultural marriage to succeed.

Jaime chose to remain in the United States not only because of his attachment to Cassie and his fear of the bad reception they would receive from his family, but also because he believed the possibilities were better there for both of them and for their child. Further, he doubted that Cassie could ever adjust to life in Santo Domingo and chose to accept the burden of being the one to adapt to the other culture.

Because Cassie had never visited Jaime's country and had little understanding of his customs, she had no way of truly understanding the sacrifices he was making or of knowing just how far he had come in adapting to her ways. She measured his behavior according to American standards, not those of his homeland. She saw no need to become familiar with any of his customs. It was bad enough, she thought, living with his "macho" attitude. She thought that it was natural that he conform to American ways, which she assumed he knew were better. Not until they made friends with another intercultural couple (Carol and Miguel) did she realize how well Jaime was coping with living in the United States and begin to see and appreciate the effort he was making.

The foreign spouse is normally the one who has to make most of the adjustments, which is fine if the foreigner likes and admires the culture of the spouse; it is miserable if this is not the case. It is one thing to know intellectually that one must adapt; it is quite another to be able to suspend judgment in the face of cultural differences which are seen as wrong. The expatriate spouse is isolated from familiar support systems, friends, and family who see and do things in the same way, who speak the same language, and with whom he or she can relax. The foreign spouse is thus disadvantaged in many ways. The home spouse, on the other hand, is surrounded by constant cultural reinforcements in the form of a familiar lifestyle and familiar objects and customs as well as old friends. The home spouse usually feels less need to alter familiar ways and expects the foreign spouse to fit in.

Probably the most difficult adjustment has to be made by the couple who meet in one spouse's country, set up a pattern of living, and then move to the other's country. Whatever the conditions in the country, the move itself may affect the relationship. Any change is difficult and stirs deep anxieties, often at an unconscious level. The couple's world gets shuffled. What worked for them before often has to be reworked in light of the ways of the new culture. Not only does the foreign spouse have new customs, living conditions, and often a new language to adjust to, but also both spouses often have to mold a new kind of personal relationship to suit the new land; they have to start over again. Perhaps the most upsetting and thorny problem is that the spouse often goes through significant personality changes upon returning home, resuming old, familiar roles.

Rosemary, an American who had met and married her Indian husband, Ravi, while both were working in Toronto, was fascinated by him and everything Indian while they were in Canada. She studied Indian history, art, language, and cooking in her enthusiasm to embrace his culture. She wore a sari whenever she entertained his many Indian friends and family who visited Toronto.

But the allure wore off when they moved in with his family in New Delhi and she saw her urbane, sophisticated husband become absorbed back into his old culture, which gradually transformed him. She nervously watched as the more passive (and in Canada repressed) aspects of his character began to reemerge. She felt isolated as he bowed to his mother's will, even in matters which she felt concerned only them as a couple. He rarely defended her from critical scrutiny or openly took her part. Because of the lack of privacy (they were always surrounded by members of his extended family), they never seemed to be able to get off by themselves to talk things through. It was as though he were the prodigal son returned home, who put on his old clothes and erased the past years—the years they had had together.

Rosemary, who already had her hands full adjusting to the move and to this difficult life, felt that Ravi was pulling away from her, falling out of love. She began to lose her self-confidence, and instead of learning to cope better as time went on, she began to function less well and to hate India for what it was doing to their marriage. She counted the days until they could move somewhere—anywhere—else. Luckily for them, Ravi was eventually assigned to Germany. Far from the eyes and influence of his own culture and strong family, Ravi readopted the ways Rosemary had known when they fell in love, and gradually things returned to normal.

On the other hand, Carol had been happy with life in Chile. She had been working in the U.S. embassy there when she met Miguel and had submitted willingly enough to the Chilean way of life, even to the male-dominant arrangement in their marriage, and she had the understanding of her colleagues at the embassy.

But when Carol was reposted to Washington, D.C., and Miguel agreed to follow, that arrangement no longer worked for them. She was embarrassed by his demanding and bossy ways in front of her old friends, and she began to feel the subtle pressure from other

Americans, who wondered aloud how she could put up with "being treated like a doormat, a second-class citizen."

Miguel didn't seem to like anything about the United States. He began praising everything about life in Chile and attacking his wife's country and its people. He criticized her friends and compatriots as "classless boors"; he disdained the "fast foods and fat asses" of people who invited them into their homes and insisted on his native cuisine in their own home. He was suspicious of her friends and work associates and was comfortable only with other Latinos, and he blatantly and openly boasted he was in America "only for the money." As she maneuvered for a position of more control in the marriage, he reacted with anger, berating her for becoming a "rampant feminist," an "emasculating woman."

Although he loved Carol, he hated her culture and refused to meet her halfway in any kind of compromise. He eventually began to identify her with everything about the country he didn't like, and she began to feel as though they had made a Latin American ghetto out of their home in her own country. She resented having to compromise her cultural heritage to try to please him. The roles which had worked in Santiago didn't in Washington. If the marriage was to be saved, the pattern of their relationship had to be modified.

Moving to a country which is home to neither spouse is considered an ideal situation for many couples in intercultural marriages. This option (alternative 3 above), however, also has its challenges, particularly if the couple is faced with substandard or vastly different living conditions, repressive laws, human rights violations, difficult climate, political unrest, manifest poverty or hunger, or a religion which dominates the lifestyle of all who live there. Simply knowing about these difficulties does not prepare people for the harsh reality of learning how to live with them. The external stress can interfere with the couple's relationship and bring about tensions.

When Cecil met and married Ikumi, he had been living in Japan for three years, spoke the language, and was familiar with and admired the ways of the land. He had studied Asian art and poetry and was comfortable with Ikumi's friends and with Asian cooking. The marriage was happy while they remained in Asia; the balance and style of the relationship remained the same.

When Cecil was recalled to England, Ikumi grieved at leaving her family but followed willingly. Although in England their life changed in that they socialized in a much different way, there were no problems because Ikumi felt at ease among Cecil's friends, who were drawn mainly from an international crowd, many of whom also had foreign wives. Basically they both did what they had always done; only the locale was different.

When Cecil was posted to Bangladesh, however, everything changed for the couple, and the strain of life in that difficult country adversely affected their relationship. There they were both foreigners, without good friends and a familiar support system, but also without the possibility of the kinds of diversions they had enjoyed in their other postings; and each reacted to the life of hardship in a different way.

Cecil threw himself into sports, amateur theatrical activities, and cocktail parties so loved by the British colonials as a means of survival "because there was nothing else to do." These, however, were not plausible survival tactics for Ikumi; she didn't care about these activities and didn't share his feelings about the empire. Instead she withdrew from others, stopped eating, complained of headaches, and became silent and remote, even from Cecil, who became frantic but at the same time resented her inability to show a "stiff upper lip." Eventually her depression became serious enough that it was thought best for her to leave the country. With shame and sadness, she returned to her parents in Japan to wait until Cecil finished his tour of duty.

Tove and Massimo had grown up with frequent moves and thrived on them; they were skilled at cross-cultural adaptation. Nevertheless, as time went on they admitted that it got more difficult; they tired of beginning all over again, losing good friends, and consoling their children, who didn't want to be uprooted another time. Still they were happiest in a culture which belonged to neither of them and where they could, within limits, make their own rules. One of their biggest concerns, however, was deciding where to "end up" after Massimo retired. They had friends everywhere and a homeland nowhere. As long as they were together, anywhere was fine, but they both worried about the day when one of them would be left behind, and they began to feel the need to find a place to put down roots.

On the other hand, putting down roots was the most contested necessity faced by Eva. She thrived on their foreign assignments, even when that meant coping with hardships and terrorists. But she hated being sent back to the United States, missed the glamour and status of the foreign postings, and hated the predictability of life in American cities. She felt their wings had been clipped when Duncan retired.

Where to live is often an issue for couples who come from different countries, and the decision may depend on what stage they are at in their lives—whether beginning their careers, schooling their children, or preparing for retirement. Often the country which they left willingly when they were young begins to lure them back as they age, and for couples who came from different countries, which one to return to can become a major problem. Or they return "home" to find that they don't belong there anymore, that they have evolved through their marriage and the passage of time and become a culture unto themselves.

9

Politics

All religions, laws, moral and political systems are but necessary means to preserve social order.
—Ch'en Ty-hsiu, "The New Youth"
(from *Sources of Chinese Tradition*,
William Theodore De Bary, ed.)

At first glance politics would seem to have little to do with love and marriage, but in intercultural marriages it intrudes if (1) the partners or their families adhere to fundamentally different political philosophies or come from historically hostile lands, (2) they are forced to live in a different country because of a political situation or because of the beliefs or practices of one of the partners, or (3) they live in a country which is in a state of war.

Just as it is unusual for two people who are zealous adherents of entirely different and mutually exclusive religions to marry, so is it unusual for partners who are each sincerely adamant believers in opposing political philosophies. This is not to say that it can't happen, but the more usual scenario is for both to live and let live or for at least one of the two to be politically flexible, open-minded, or indifferent, giving way to the persuasion of the more dominant one. For example, Brazilian Maria Clotilde, to use her own words, "couldn't have cared less" about global affairs unless they touched on her daily life, while her husband, Zoahar, was a dedicated pacifist who devoted his professional and personal time and gave donations to pacifist and human rights movements. Although different in their interests, they were compatible. Politics was not a problem for them.

Some couples seem politically farther apart than they really are. Bejeweled and befurred Fiamma, who claimed membership in the Italian Communist party (renamed Democratic Party of the Left), was more verbally opposed to the capitalist views of her English husband, Andrew, than she was in actuality; she liked the shock her ideology caused in bourgeois circles but never let the party philosophy interfere with the jet-set lifestyle they both enjoyed. Andrew, on the other hand, admittedly believed in nothing; he considered all governments equally corrupt and was amused by his "comrade wife in sable," who alternately defended the rights of the worker and sent back the wine at the Tour d'Argent.

Couples with sincere political differences, however, can have problems. Chilean Miguel and American Carol, for example, were both politically involved and poles apart in their beliefs. It was useless for them to say they were going to keep politics out of their marriage. They felt the strain of their different affiliations and beliefs, whichever country they lived in. In Chile, although Carol had managed to accommodate to the Chilean lifestyle, she still worked for the American embassy and found it difficult to represent her country and associate with Miguel and his anti-American friends at the same time. These were the days when General Pinochet, who had assumed power in a military coup, ruled the country by decree. It was a time of severe anti-American feelings. Carol's boss was not pleased with her impending marriage to a "high-risk, host country national," and Miguel's friends saw his association with her as an affront to their cause. Opposition came at them from all angles.

Much as they tried to keep encounters purely social, politics crept in. It became difficult for them to meet either with his friends or with her friends (never both together) without tempers flaring and feelings being hurt. More and more the two of them went out alone together, isolating themselves in order to avoid conflict, which found a way of intruding on their personal relationship. Miguel began to be ostracized by his more radical companions, and Carol started to avoid her American friends. As much as they told themselves that having to overcome these obstacles to be together would only strengthen their love, the strain was evident.

To a certain extent, intercultural couples marry the fate of the partner's land. In 1995 the story of Jennifer Harbury and Efrain Bamaca Velasquez made headlines. She, a Harvard-educated, American lawyer on a trip to Guatemala to research human rights violations, met and married Bamaca, a Mayan peasant turned leftist guerrilla. The story of their brief and improbable-sounding marriage is one which is totally entwined with his country's (and her country's) politics. Together in the United States for a few brief months after being married, they were separated in 1992 when he returned to Guatemala and shortly thereafter disappeared. While she fought for three years to learn of his fate (undertaking hunger strikes in front of the White House and the National Palace in Guatemala City), he lay dead, presumably a victim of a Guatemalan military officer—who was also a CIA-paid agent.[1]

Helga, the youthful German rebel and wife of the Libyan radical, was eventually forced to leave Libya with her children and move to Geneva because of her husband's political activities. Although she discarded many of her own radical views once she moved to Tripoli and had children, she was not able to escape Libyan politics. Living in Tripoli was dangerous. In addition, her husband was active in the underground, and sometimes days went by without her hearing from him. She knew better than to ask questions, but she lived in a near constant state of panic. She recalls days when she combed the hospitals and prisons, placing money in the right hands for information when he had been missing for longer than usual. She lived in fear for him and for herself and their children.

Helga is but one of the many intercultural spouses to find themselves living in a third country because of politics, but some are not simply waiting for their spouses; they are outcasts, often permanent outcasts.

Adela and Mohammed, who met and married in Philadelphia, were attracted to one another in part by the similarity of their homeless condition; one was a refugee from Cuba; the other, from Iran. Depending on which country was in the news at the time, they suf-

---

[1] "The End of the Vigil," *Time*, 3 April 1995.

fered alternately from anti–Cuban and anti–Arab prejudices, although they were in Philadelphia precisely because they did not agree with what was going on in their countries and felt compelled to leave. During the Gulf War, for example, and when Cuban boat people were flooding Miami, they felt singled out for attention and even received anonymous harassing phone calls. Things usually died down, the calls were from a few fanatics, but it still left them feeling vulnerable. Fear was a constant emotion.

Adela explained that women who marry into another culture also assume the nationality and must shoulder the prejudices people have toward that culture: "When there are problems with Cuban refugees, I am Cuban, but I become Arab because of my marriage whenever there are terrorist activities anywhere in the Middle East. It's hard enough for both of us to have to live in a country not our own, far away from those we have left behind, worrying about their well-being and safety, living our lives in one land but attached with invisible ties and loyalties to the ones we left, but to be identified with our enemies is almost unbearable."

A political situation also affected the lives of Harry and Milee. After the fall of Saigon, they were not at peace until they managed to assist her family in relocating to Australia, which meant actually taking in her entire family (mother, father, siblings, and grandmother) and assuming responsibility for their travel expenses, clothing, and food and for finding them jobs, homes, and schools. Over a ten-year period, two or three of her Vietnamese relatives lived with them at a time, draining their finances and straining their intimate family lifestyle. Harry found himself "surrounded by a foreign colony" that spoke a language he didn't speak and cooked food he didn't like in what was left of his own home. He and Milee often took long walks just to be alone together.

Although he did not regret what they did, he was glad when it was over and he and his wife were on their own, finally able to permit themselves a few extras: a new car, a family vacation, a bank account with something in it.

A similar story is told by Annamaria, an Argentinian woman, and Erol, her Bosnian husband, who met and married in the United States. When the former Yugoslavia disintegrated and Bosnia was being destroyed by interethnic warfare, they were in touch with some of his distant relatives who were living under siege in Sarajevo. These relatives had learned that they might be able to get visas to the United States because *their* mixed marriages put them in the "high risk" category: the families consisted of twin sisters who were Catholics married to Muslim men. In prewar Sarajevo this was not an uncommon occurrence, as the city was one in which Jews, Catholics, Muslims, and Russian Orthodox studied, lived, and worked amicably side by side. With the new nationalism, however, these couples, and especially their mixed children, no longer fit or felt safe. As they explained, "People must declare their identity, and these children, who are mixed, are no longer considered pure. There is no future for them there, except the possibility of persecution." Consequently they were able to get visas for the United States.

But getting into the United States was not enough for people who had to leave their jobs and all their possessions behind. And so Annamaria and Erol came to the rescue, offering the extra rooms in their home to seven people who were practically strangers, helping them learn English, guiding them through the intricacies of learning to integrate into a new culture, and buoying them up when the memories of the hardships and atrocities they had witnessed as well as thoughts of those they had left behind came back to haunt them. Their lives changed overnight, but as Annamaria said, "How could we not be there to help them?"

Politics can also intrude into the relationship of couples when their countries are long-term enemies. Because of the physical proximity of the two nations, marriages between Palestinians and Israelis are not uncommon. But whenever hostilities between the two peoples flare up, these Romeo–Juliet couples are caught in the middle. The problems in their marriage come not from within, but often from the families and society surrounding them. Another example is the marriages between Estonians and Russians, which occur because of the long occupation of Estonia by the Russians. Such marriages are disparaged by Estonians (who, because of long-standing resentment, have also made it difficult for Russians to be full-fledged citizens).

The adjustment of the intercultural couple is also affected by the political climate of their chosen country. If this climate includes hostility toward the country of one of the partners, a violent or repressive government, civil war, racial tension, terrorist activities, or instability, the marriage may be in for some hard times.

When Deirdre married Mario, it never occurred to her that life would be much different; after all, she was going to a Western European country. When they moved to Rome in the 1970s, she was more than enthusiastic about the life she led there. The few inconveniences—the strikes which regularly stopped essential services, the student protests, the occasional terrorist attacks on public places—seemed a small price to pay for living in that beautiful country. None of it really touched her deeply. It actually bothered Mario more. He was more critical of his fellow Italians than his wife was. She could, after all, consider the Italians "them," not "us," and take a philosophical attitude toward the whole thing. "A little tear gas here and there, but I got used to it," she said.

But like Helga in Libya, after their children were born these things bothered her more, and the tension increased. She actually knew some of the people who were kidnapped; a friend of theirs was a victim of an airport bomb; and the children went to the American school on buses which were inspected daily by armed police and specially trained dogs. Fear became a common companion; people stopped going out much; the streets were deserted by 10:30 at night; the women put away their furs and stopped carrying handbags for fear of being accosted; and the men were armed with guns.

It wasn't fun anymore, and gradually the situation began to wear on her nerves and on Mario's (who went to work at the bank in an armored car, taking a different route every day so as not to be a target for the unknown, unseen assailant). They, their children, and their friends lived in a controlled but constant state of tension. They were afraid to pick up the newspaper for fear of reading about the latest public outrage. Some people left the country; others transferred their money across the border into Switzerland. Uncertainty became their daily diet, and Deirdre began to wonder whether it was worth it.

Duncan and Eva and their six children lived in constant tension because of the activities of the Tupamaros, who targeted Duncan while he was consul in Puerta Allegre, Brazil. The children thought life there was exciting and made a game out of ditching their bodyguards, but

Eva, who already by nature ran a tight ship, had to enforce even more strict discipline on the children and at the same time avoid being overly protective or frightening them.

A hardship post can be a strain on a marriage, as was learned by Italian diplomat Massimo and his wife, Tove, when they were posted to Beijing. The ability to adapt to a politically repressive environment depends on the personal makeup of the individual as well as on the length of stay. Although these two world travelers took it pretty much in stride, they saw the marriages of many of their fellow sojourners suffer. "Anyone can stand it for a while," Tove explained, "but after three years, one's sense of humor and sense of good sportsmanship wane and life drags interminably from one vacation or home leave to the next."

Life in countries with repressive but stable governments poses other kinds of problems for the intercultural spouse. Living where people are not free to move around as they like, where dissenters whisper their conversations for fear of being overheard, where telephones are monitored and mail is opened, and where newspapers are censored and homes randomly searched can be suffocating, affecting the harmony of the family, especially for those raised in a free country.

10

Friends

The fortunate man has bread and friends.

—Korean Proverb

Friendship is a basic need of human beings. Finding a friend, someone with whom one has shared sensibilities, is important, even within
one's own culture. In many respects it parallels the marital relationship in that its success depends on two people having the same background, interests, and values. All cultures value friendship and all
couples need friends, but finding and maintaining them often pre-
sents unique problems for intercultural couples.

The reasons are many. For one thing, cultures have their own
definitions of what constitutes friendship and different rules regarding fostering and maintaining their friendships. Americans, for example, have categories of people they call friends, some of whom are
easily acquired and often just as easily discarded. Many Europeans
associate only within their own social circle. Latin Americans and
Middle Easterners consider friends as quasi-kin who can be counted
on for anything and who will never let them down. Often people of
one culture do not understand (or they disagree with) the other's
conception of the meaning of "friendship" and may feel that they do
not have any "true" friends from the other culture. For example, one
American woman, accustomed to friendships which respect the
individual's privacy, found the friends of her Palestinian spouse "invasive people who take advantage of us"; her Palestinian spouse felt
slighted and offended by what he saw as indifference on the part of

their American friends who "wait to be asked" before they offer needed help.

Another problem commonly experienced by intercultural couples is that, while they themselves may have adjusted to the many cultural differences between them, their friends may not have been able or willing to and may be unaccepting of the foreign partner. They may have been against the marriage in the first place, adhering to basic beliefs of "like marries like," quoting proverbs such as "Moglie e buoi, paese tuoi" (Get your cattle and your wives from your own land). Bill and Mary found that some of their old friends in both the United States and Nigeria objected to their interracial marriage (feeling that they had betrayed their race by needing to find a man or woman of another) and turned against them. They had to find new friends as a couple, people who not only were receptive to their marriage but didn't consider it anything out of the ordinary.

Even couples whose friends do not disapprove of the marriage often find that their same-culture friends are uncomfortable around their spouses. The situation is further complicated if there is a language barrier. The friends must slow down, repeat, and explain, which makes for stilted socializing. Worse yet, they sometimes ignore the foreigner's presence.

Jaime, who believed that American friendships are facile and superficial ("Americans say 'hi, how are you?' without it meaning anything. They don't care how you are."), also had trouble communicating with Cassie's friends. He resented the fact that when they laughed and joked around, they did not always take care to be sure he understood. He often got to the point where he stopped trying, tuned them out, then claimed that no one noticed. Or, worse, he would interrupt them in midsentence with something he was thinking—which had nothing to do with what they were discussing—and he would be seen as rude. He was hurt when Cassie defended her friends, saying that they were uncomfortable around him because they weren't sure whether he liked or approved of them. They saw his tuning out as aloofness.

Jaime also had problems with Cassie's insistence on keeping her former male friends. Much as he tried to believe her claim that "in Chicago, men and women can be *just* friends, without any sexual connotations," it went against his nature; he didn't like it, and he didn't want his wife having such friends. But in their American social circle he was alone in this belief, which only made him more intransigent. It was one of the disagreements they never satisfactorily resolved.

Friends are needed not only as an outlet or cushion for moments of stress or conflict, which even the happiest marriages encounter, but also as a touchstone of one's own reality. One American woman, happily married to a Persian and living in Finland, talked about missing the kind of friends with whom she could "cut loose, dress like a bag lady, be a little crazy" and said her only outlet was when "I turn on The Temptations full blast in my home and dance with the vacuum cleaner."

Yvette had a similar feeling when she and Ali moved back to Kuwait. Earlier, when they were living in London, they both had friends of many nationalities drawn from the foreign student population of the university; nevertheless, as a couple they associated primarily with Ali's friends. Yvette had French women friends, whom she saw alone. Basically, it was a satisfactory arrangement.

Ali's friends were invariably courteous to her and fun to be around. If she had any complaint, it was that they were around a little too much—she and Ali had little time alone together. But she accepted Ali's explanation that in his culture people don't apply time limits (or any other kind of limits) to friendships. As Yvette saw it, this meant no privacy and no personal property—what was theirs was everyone's. This was not an easy thing for her to accept, but she felt guilty and selfish complaining about it.

When Ali finished his degree, they married and moved to Kuwait, where Yvette was thrown off balance by suddenly being deprived of the outlet provided by her women friends, who saw things as she did and by being just as suddenly surrounded by people who saw the world as Ali did.

In addition, she found that many of the same men who had camped in their apartment in London and who had interacted with her freely, enjoying political and religious discussions, now treated her with deference, ignoring her after the first social amenities and leaving her to the women—who, for the most part, bored her. "They are sweet," she said, "I just have nothing to say to them, nor have they ever really accepted me as one of them."

The need for a close, same-sex friend, "someone with whom to exchange impressions of my life in this new country, someone who would understand my doubts, fears, problems as well as my enthusiasms, and at the same time sympathetically set me straight when I was off track" was a need expressed by Rosemary as well during her years in India. Ravi was going through reentry shock and wrestling with the changes demanded of him as he readapted to India, and both of them were struggling with what it meant to their relationship. Feeling distanced from him, she had no one to turn to or confide in. She also bemoaned the difficulty they had in finding couples they both could relate to. "There were intercultural couples where we were living, but although the women were foreign and the husbands Indian, the women were rarely from my same background or nationality, and the men were often not from the same Indian subculture as my husband. So, in the end we had little in common."

Dorrie, with the fair complexion and blond hair so typical of her Dutch compatriots, also experienced isolation when she and her Japanese husband returned to Tokyo after she finished her graduate work.

> Because we Western women so obviously look different, we stand out, and in reality are left out. In our case, because Hiroshi and I both moved in the academic world, I was accepted, but being accepted is not the same thing as having a good, close friend. I personally like to be open and informal and find that I cannot—must not—be myself in Japan. After a while that gets tiresome and I long for the casual kind of relationship I can have with people of my own country.

This is the reason, she explained, that many of the foreign women belong to associations like the Foreign Wives of Japanese, which serves as a link between cultures. "It is in these groups that we can find empathetic friends as well as learn about the people and local customs from the old-timers."

Many couples find that they get along best with other intercultural couples, not only because they share some of the same experiences and problems, but because they are better able to empathize with the delicate and difficult balance these couples have managed to achieve in their marriages. Such couples usually know how not to intrude and also can serve as sounding boards for one another, sharing the mutuality of problems not experienced by same-culture couples.

Like Yvette and Rosemary, Rashida was touched by the sincere, open warmth of the women when she moved to Kenya, but she also knew she was not like them and felt separate. She depended a great deal on her friendship with other African American women who, like her, had married Kenyan men. "We were lifesavers to one another, talked the same shorthand, and shared the common bond of nationality as well as state of frustration and confusion. We were truly sisters." Their husbands also benefited from being able to share with each other experiences with their foreign wives.

Harry, however, did not know many other men with foreign wives in Melbourne and felt he was sinking in a sea of misunderstanding with his Vietnamese wife "for what seemed like years." Milee admitted quite frankly that she did not have any real friends who were not Asian-born: "I like the Australians, but they cannot be my true friends. We are too different." At first Harry was upset by her failure to integrate fully into life in Australia and form any close friendships among his people, but at the same time he was relieved when she finally met a Japanese woman who introduced her to a group of other Asian wives because he saw how badly she needed their companionship. Then, of course, when her family arrived from Vietnam after the fall of Saigon, she associated primarily with them.

Not only could Milee not relate to Harry's blunt, outspoken friends, she also had problems understanding Harry's way of relating to his friends. She resented the physicality of the people, the touching and punching that went on between men and women, finding it distasteful and unnecessarily intimate. She had trouble accepting the way he "mistreated" his good friends when they were guests in their home, engaging in loud, frank arguments, pointed, intrusive questions, sarcasm, and teasing, which she found totally lacking in sensitivity and courtesy.

Differences in styles of entertaining can also be disturbing. Barbara Telser-Gadow found in her study of Iranian/U.S. couples that Americans and Iranians had quite different ideas about socializing. Americans felt that Iranians generally overdid their entertaining, "making a big production out of it," while the Iranians felt that the Americans were inhospitable, taking their friends out to restaurants rather than entertaining them at home. Americans have a social relationship only with their TVs, the Iranians sniffed.[1]

Friends, and the concept of friendship, can be a big issue for intercultural couples and, in some ways, one that causes frequent disagreement. Finding a way to live with these differences is critical because having friends is important not only for the individuals but for the marriage as well. An isolated couple is neither a happy nor a healthy couple. Friendships can keep the partners from becoming too isolated or dependent on one another, which may eventually come to mean having too much of each other's company.

Perhaps the ideal solution, such as that eventually worked out between Milee and Harry, is for both partners to have, as Harry explained,

> lots of different kinds of friends. I have my friends—from work, from tennis or old school connections, and she has her friends, and we have our friends. Sometimes we get together with the husbands of her friends or the wives of my friends or have Esperanto parties all together. We don't both get along with everybody, but that's all right because each of us separately and both of us together have managed, with a lot of trial and error, to fill in the gaps.

---

[1] Barbara Telser-Gadow, "Intercultural Communication Competence in Intercultural Marriages," thesis, University of Minnesota, 1992, 102-04.

11

Finances

Money is the sinew of love as well as of war.
—Thomas Fuller, *Gnomonologia*

In all marriages, monocultural and intercultural alike, financial issues can be a source of major disagreement. Financial problems, however, are often seen as more numerous and tougher to solve in intercultural marriages because these couples seem to need more money to keep their international lives afloat. As well, they often have culturally based differences regarding such matters as who earns the money and who controls its expenditure; how much should be spent and how much saved; and what kinds of things it should be spent on (personal pleasure, children, relatives, etc.) Different value orientations are involved and different priorities must be considered by intercultural partners, and indeed, it may take more money to keep such a marriage going smoothly because of the diverse needs and desires of the partners. Some couples believe that both personal and financial resources are integral to the success of these marriages. Many recall how much less tolerant of each other they were early in the marriage, when money was limited and closer quarters and necessary budgetary sacrifices made every difference seem more exasperating than it might later on, when increased affluence meant more money to go around, permitting greater acceptance of one another's "quirks and manias."

Who earns the money in the family can be a male-female role issue. In some cultures—even where they have newly won legal rights to control their property—women have little say in managing finances, are totally dependent upon their husbands, and must ask permission for every expense. In others, it is the woman who takes the husband's paycheck and is responsible for managing all the family finances.

Earning money is often an exclusively male role. In Latin cultures the traditional husband who can afford it wants his wife at home, and though today the necessity of two-income families is breaking down this type of role division, it has not disappeared.

Mario, for example, did everything he could to sabotage Deirdre's attempts to pick up the career she had left when she married and followed him to Italy. "The evils of the world stem from the woman who works," he told her, implying that she would inevitably fail in her true role as wife and mother if she did less than devote herself exclusively to home and family. He also always managed to minimize the importance of her work; as far as he was concerned, it could be interrupted or put aside if he had a more pressing "need" for her attention. This really upset her, but because the income her work brought in was modest, she was never able to convince him that her career was important.

Even Jaime, who recognized that they couldn't get by without Cassie's paycheck, felt less a man because of his working wife and promised himself that as soon as he got a decent job he would make her quit and stay home with Jennifer. Obviously, her full-time job did not release her from any of the domestic duties traditionally associated with women.

Sune, on the other hand, who came from Sweden, was often frustrated at being the sole wage earner; but he was never able to convince his Malaysian wife, Rani, that she might help out. She was shocked that he was not proud to be able to support a wife who stayed at home. She had not been prepared to do anything else. Although she complained ceaselessly about not having enough money, working was out of the question for her.

Sometimes the argument is over how much money is saved, how much is spent immediately, and how it is spent. Although this issue depends for the most part on the individual personalities involved, it can also be a cultural issue. One Japanese wife (who held as sacred the maxim that one must begin each new year free of debt) was disconcerted by her American husband's casual use of credit cards and his extensive borrowing. A British man berated his American wife for her apparent "need to trade in perfectly good things for new ones." He saw this "obsession with newness" as ostentation rather than good taste.

Maria Clotilde and Zoahar, who had different ideas about how they wanted to live their lives, also had divergent ideas on how to spend their money. As a good Brazilian Carioca, she knew that life was to be lived and enjoyed, and she had little patience with her driven Israeli husband.

Zoahar, who had known poverty and insecurity, felt that a good bank account was his only defense against the unknown future. He found Maria Clotilde's attitude frivolous and kept close tabs on how she spent the money he doled out to her. He was also an inveterate bargain hunter and would become irate when she would give in to impulse buying or pay full price for things. They had very different ideas about what constituted needs versus luxuries in the areas of food, clothing, and housing. What she considered essentials, he considered extras. She felt life was not worth living without dining out and dancing; he thought these were frivolities. While she spent money on hairdressers, dressmakers, and phone calls to her family and friends in Rio de Janeiro, he made donations to political or charitable causes and invested in growth stocks. Their money arguments were never-ending.

A common intercultural issue stemming from how money should be spent is that of the extent of financial responsibility a spouse feels for friends and extended family. Milee and Harry were fortunate in that he understood that she had a filial duty to her parents, instilled in her by her culture, and that she would never be happy, no matter how little money they had to spend on themselves, until her family was safely settled close by her. Telling himself it would not be forever, he made her priorities his and worked to help her family until all of them were safe. Still there were times when he wondered when they would be able to save some of his hard-earned money for their own future.

Although Adela as a Cuban understood and shared her Iranian husband's sense of loyalty to his family and friends and took pride in being able to share his success, she resented the fact that there were no limits placed on what they could afford to share, and there was rarely any money left over for themselves. The others always came first—there was always another brother to put through school; the gifts they gave were never too expensive. She felt that his Iranian friends took advantage of him as well and finally persuaded him to curtail some of his monetary assistance. As a result Mohammed lost prestige with his friends, who felt that he had been contaminated by his foreign wife and the American culture in which he lived.

Cecil understood Ikumi's need to return home to see her family and reimmerse herself in her own culture once in a while and felt that the money for her trips was well spent. But when their son was ready for boarding school, he couldn't afford to support both her frequent trips and an expensive school. Despite her lamentations that she did not want the boy to go away from home for school, the English boarding school won out. However, with both her parents and her son far away, the phone bills went up, and despite his complaints, this was something Cecil had to accept.

While Deirdre felt that trips to visit family took priority in their budgeting, Mario insisted on the more luxurious status vacations which enabled him to maintain *bella figura* among his friends. Since it was almost impossible for them to manage both, for the sake of compromise Deirdre let the chic hotels and "in" resorts win out, though they meant less to her than they did to him.

Olu took it as one more sign that his wife was not a proper woman when Rashida complained that her own paycheck from the school where she gave voice lessons was used to help out his extended family, a matter about which she was given little say. Things became even more tense when their sons (under their mother's tutelage) questioned why the grandmothers and cousins were given preference over them. Finally, Rashida managed to get the school to give her two paychecks, one which would be used for her in-laws and a second secret one which served for her and her sons.

When money is unlimited, the priorities of both partners can generally be satisfied (both partners willing), but when it is not, there are choices to be made. As Dorrie put it, "Every foreign spouse should have some *hesso-kuri*, which literally translates as 'honorable funds

hidden in belly button,' for psychological independence, emergen-
cies, travel to the homeland, medical problems, and also, of course, in
case the marriage ends."

12

In-Laws

> Happiness is having a large, loving, caring, close-knit family in another city.
>
> —George Burns

Families are not something young men and women shed upon marrying, but usually something they acquire more of. In an intercultural marriage, not only does the couple get a set of foreign in-laws; they may also wed a totally absorbing concept of family which will have a great bearing on how they live their married lives.

In certain cultures (for example, Anglo-Saxon) parents normally begin educating their children at an early age to accept responsibility for their actions and then push them out of the nest as soon as they can stand on their own two feet. They avoid invading their children's privacy once they have reached adulthood, and they themselves often settle into retirement colonies or old people's homes when they are no longer able to care for themselves.

In other cultures (Asian, Middle Eastern, African, for example) parents never really let go of their children. They maintain patriarchal authority and do not expect to be abandoned in their old age. They devote themselves to their children when they are small but have power over them and expect eternal respect and loyalty from them when they are grown. The family tie does not decrease; it extends when a son or daughter marries.

These cultural differences make for quite diverse interpretations of how to handle and relate to in-laws. More often than in monocultural marriages, parents may strongly disapprove of the child's choice of a spouse. While initially pulling the couple closer in mutual self-defense, parental opposition in the long run can precipitate conflict and distrust.

Even before marriage, in-laws can pose a threat to the couple. When Cecil and Ikumi decided to marry, her family was devastated and did everything in its power to break up the relationship. Despite Cecil's upright character and good position, the parents, and even Ikumi's brother, looked upon her marriage to a foreigner as an unforgivable act that would bring shame on the family. Furthermore, as Ikumi's mother explained to Cecil, "One of the main reasons for marriage is to have children who will care for you in your old age. If you take my daughter away, I have no one." At one point they controlled their daughter's activities to keep the couple from meeting and tried to pay Cecil to leave the country.

This reaction, while extreme, is not rare for parents of intercultural couples (although many others manage to marry with the blessings of both sets of parents). Bill and Mary experienced the same kind of resistance to their marriage. His family had accepted and understood Bill's involvement in civil rights issues during and after his college days and had even encouraged him to join the Peace Corps. But they felt he had gone too far when he brought home a bride who was not only from another country (Nigeria) but of another race, and they could not accept the marriage. "We're not racists," they insisted, "but with all the problems there are in a marriage between two people, you have no business adding another dimension." Mary's family was no less horrified. To them the world was divided into black and white, and she had joined the enemy. They wanted no part of the young couple.

Planning the wedding ceremony itself often brings out the worst in the families and can test the strength of the relationship of the couple. Heated arguments often occur over the kind of service (religious or not; his, hers, or a blend); the wedding attire (traditional or modern; his or hers, or both); the wedding reception(s) (which will honor both sides equally and accommodate a cultural array of guests); and the kind of food offered (a ten-course Chinese banquet or American buffet.) Many couples relate that sorting out the wedding-planning differences brought them to the brink of breaking up as they realized not only how intransigent their families could be, but also how tied they themselves were to their cultural traditions and family values. Others claim the wedding is a good place to start a dialogue on these matters, and still others opt for a small civil wedding far away from family interference.

Even when the families have accepted the marriage there is frequently a standoff period while they wait to see how well the new son- or daughter-in-law will conform to their ways. They often take subtle (or not so subtle) measures designed to influence the behavior of the newlyweds, sometimes undermining the solidity of the young couple's unity.

Rosemary, for example, waged a continuing battle with her mother-in-law over the question of Ravi's primary allegiance. While she understood, abstractly, that his culture called for stronger ties to his family and greater deference to his mother's will than was the case in her own culture, when his family took precedence over their personal relationship, she was resentful and fought back. She also struggled to retain her independence from her mother-in-law, who attempted to transform her into an exemplary subservient daughter-in-law. This constant tug-of-war posed many problems for the couple, especially for Rosemary, during their years in India and was resolved only by their transfer out of the country.

But it was not easy for Ravi either, who had his own in-laws to deal with. Having grown up accustomed to the Indian way of being able to count on the extended family for whatever needs might arise, he had to act otherwise when dealing with Rosemary's parents, who were self-sufficient and expected their children to be so as well. It was one thing for the two of them to know intellectually the difference in the two families (that with one they *had* to be dependent and with the other, avoid being so), but it was quite another to relate properly to both without dissonance.

The difference in attitude can be illustrated by the story told by one American mother whose son married a Japanese girl and who made every effort to stay out of the young couple's way and not get involved in their disagreements. Much to her surprise, when the marriage between the couple did not work out, she was blamed by her daughter-in-law for not having been a good mother-in-law because she did not teach her son's wife how to properly care for him. The mother-in-law was at fault for not interfering!

The family can, of course, also be the couple's best ally, its staunchest supporter, willing to help when needed and strong when the couple is having problems. Often it is they who will step in and assist the foreign spouse or help resolve disputes between the couple. Yvette found that the women of Ali's family secretly admired and envied her egalitarian relationship with her husband and encouraged her to maintain it within their own culture. "My mother-in-law is a closet feminist," Yvette confided, "and while I find that I don't have a lot to say to her and her daughters beyond home and family, their warmth and 'secret support' have more than compensated for it."

Even Ali's father accepted her ways—as long as she bowed to his absolute authority over the entire family. In fact, the two of them had a very special relationship not afforded to the Kuwaiti daughters-in-law, wives of Ali's brothers, because she was a foreigner. If she respected the family's ways, she found them very accepting; they were delighted to teach her their customs and their cooking, and to help out whenever needed. "I have been enveloped in the warmth of their understanding, acceptance, and kindness," she stated, "which has helped me overcome inevitable bouts of homesickness."

Milee, on the other hand, had a problem with the exuberant warmth and welcome she received from Harry's Australian family. While she understood their sincerity, these were not her ways, and instinctively she drew back and unwittingly offended them. Harry found himself acting as a constant go-between, explaining to his family that her reserve was not repugnance and explaining to her that their teasing ways were not meant to be invasive or rude.

Close family involvement can also smother or burden an intercultural marriage, particularly when one partner is not used to a demanding family relationship. Compatibility issues crop up not only with the parents-in-law but frequently also with siblings of the spouse. Siblings who have grown up very close to one another are often less tolerant of cultural differences, and they are sometimes resentful of the changes brought about by the foreign spouse and outspoken in their observations.

Although Ikumi's parents, for example, eventually did come around and accept her marriage to Cecil, her brother did not; he and Cecil were like oil and water, disliking and criticizing each other, making family reunions painful, and causing Ikumi to feel torn in her loyalties.

Jaime's family was also initially unable to fully accept Cassie, whom they did not consider of their same class. When Jennifer was born, however, all was forgiven, and Cassie became a member of the family—with all that it involved.

After the marriage, a stream of Jaime's relatives began to arrive in Chicago for prolonged stays. One brother lived with them for over a year, which strained the couple's meager budget and put an almost unbearable strain on their relationship. Jaime placed no limits on their welcome, nor on how much he did for them. He became a different person, as far as Cassie could see, showing off when they were around, reverting to the macho behavior expected of a man in his culture and attempting to extract deferential behavior from Cassie, which had nothing to do with the kind of relationship they had established. Cassie, in turn, became more confrontational and willful. The presence of the resident relatives threw their entire relationship out of kilter, changed the atmosphere of their home, and frayed their tempers.

Olu's large family was wonderful to Rashida when she came to live in Kenya; and though she had trouble learning to accept their interference in the couple's affairs, she found that they were able to mediate the arguments between the two of them, just as they often unwittingly caused them. But it went against her grain to be so entwined with the extended family, who considered themselves "other mothers and fathers" to the boys, and to accept that her husband felt his duties to his family came before his duties to his wife and sons.

Daniele explained how important it is in collective cultures (like that of Morocco, where she lived) for the family to be supportive: "Love cannot be separated from the context of the family. As foreign wives with our own families far away, we join our husband's family and they can make or break the marriage."

Some couples find that their marital survival depends on the distance they keep from both sets of in-laws and so choose to live in a third country, where they are free to live their own lives and resolve their own problems. But running away, as some couples view it, can be a lonely, incomplete answer, because it doesn't really solve anything. Both spouses cut themselves off not only from their pasts but also from their support systems. Distance brings with it other problems as well. Many spouses who live far away from their families find themselves confronted with difficult decisions to make when elderly parents become ill or infirm.

After her father died, Lynn, married to Hans and living in Austria, had to decide what to do with her mother, who was suffering from Alzheimer's disease. It was a difficult and costly decision, but they finally elected to move her mother to a home for the elderly in New York, reconciling Lynn's conscience by making frequent and expensive trips back and forth between countries to check on her well-being.

Mary, who lived in Berkeley, California, far from her parents in Nigeria, knew the desperation of being distant from loved ones when her father fell ill and his days were numbered.

Her brothers and sisters said, "Come now," but that was impossible. Mary's daughter was in the hospital and needed her. It was no use saying Bill could take over; he had a full-time job, one which took him all over the country. There was no extended family to fall back on as there would have been in Nigeria, no one who could help out. Her duties were *here*, now, to her immediate family.

"Tell him to wait," she begged her mother over the phone. "I'll get there somehow. Don't let him die." She was torn between her two families. Her father did hang on until she was able to reach his bedside weeks later, but some expatriate spouses never see their parents again, and this can be one of their greatest sacrifices.

In sum, close family involvement is a double-edged sword; the extended family can be the couple's best ally or the couple's worst enemy, confusing involvement with interference, invading the couple's privacy, and perhaps instigating arguments and causing problems. Although some couples bond more closely as a reaction against nonsupportive parents, others say that external problems which arise because of one family or the other cause them more conflict than any other issue.

13

Social Class

A man's manners are a mirror in which he shows his portrait.

—Goethe, *Proverbs in Prose*

Some people, including some cross-cultural couples, maintain that an intercultural marriage is no more complicated or difficult than a monocultural one as long as both partners come from the same social strata of their respective countries.

While this is an oversimplification of the matter, it is true that class counts. Similar social background is an important ingredient in any marriage, intercultural or not, as it implies (but does not guarantee) similarity of education, attitudes, tastes, and manners. However, there seems to be more crossing of classes in intercultural marriages than in monocultural ones. There are various explanations for this, many of them tied to the motivations behind the marriage. Rebels, for example (remember our typologies in the first chapter), tend to react against their culture or their personal background in choosing a spouse. Lynn, for instance, wanted to be freed from the suburban trap of her upbringing and was attracted to Hans in part because he was so different from the young men she had dated. Helga, who met her activist Libyan husband as a result of her own political activities, was swept off her feet by this romantic who was so different from her proper physics professor father.

More often, however, the couples are merely unaware of their class differences. They simply don't know enough about their partner's culture to be able to assess his or her status within it. Often one of the partners has never been to the other's country to see the culture in action; therefore one partner has no idea what is and is not acceptable behavior in the other's society and so attributes a lot of questionable behavior to foreignness rather than to class differences.

As Yvette explained it, "I forgave him all sorts of things I'd never let a French guy get away with because I thought that was just the way they did things in his country. Was I mad when I found out that in some ways he was a boor even in his own language."

Frequently, the failure to recognize class differences happens because the young people meet on neutral ground in a third country where they are foreigners, coping with the ways of a land which is strange to both of them, making mistakes, and sometimes expressing themselves haltingly and incorrectly, sometimes in a language neither of them speaks fluently.

Often couples meet on a university campus, where a student ghetto-like atmosphere prevails. Everyone dresses alike and uses the same, currently popular modes of expression and behavior, which might be quite different from what they would use at home. There may be little interaction with older adults other than university personnel (who don't count, as they reflect student styles as well). When the couple meets, both are playing the role of student and are often quite different people from what they are at home. There is an egalitarian spirit and atmosphere.

When they return to their own country, however, they revert to familiar roles, habits, and patterns of behavior. The bride or groom brought to the new home may be in for a few surprises. The family may or may not be what had been portrayed. In their limbo-like courtship neither one of them probably gave—or was able to give—an accurate description of what "back home" was like.

Much the same thing happens when servicemen marry women of the country where they are stationed. Often loneliness overcomes common sense, and the soldier marries the first woman he meets, knowing next to nothing about her or the culture of her country. The woman often doesn't have any real idea about his family or background until they return to his homeland and she sees him out of uniform and interacting with his relatives and friends.

One Korean war bride, who was raised in the city of Seoul but ended up in the heart of Kansas farmland, was so distressed by what she had done that upon arrival in her husband's modest, isolated home, she took to her room and didn't eat or leave it for a week. In time the innate kindness of the family won her over, but she had to learn to live in a social setting and with people of a background different from her own, to understand different behavior, and to associate with a class of people she would never have known in her own land.

Sometimes the shock is in discovering that the mother-in-law is illiterate and squats on the floor to do the cooking, as was the case with Victor from Switzerland. Or one finds that the spouse comes from less educated people who believe in stricter enforcement of gender roles or maintain rigid religious observation. Others may find that the family has unexpected formal codes of behavior by which the new spouse will be judged. Cross-culturally appropriate behavior (dress, topics of conversation, etc.) is often hard to intuit accurately, making it stressful for the expat spouse, who may make dreadful gaffes, embarrassing or humiliating the home spouse, who is left to explain.

Visiting the spouse's country before the marriage may not help either, since the partner may not speak the language (or doesn't speak it well) and so misses telltale speech patterns, accents, and grammatical slipups, which would give some indication of background. Even those who have spent some time in their spouse's homeland and have some knowledge of the language have only been visitors, and so are likely to have had few intimate contacts with the people. As a result, their understanding of status delineations or subtle class distinctions is likely to be severely limited, and they will often totally miss those aspects of their prospective partner's speech and behavior which would give them the clues they need. It takes time to figure out where people really belong in another society because each culture has its own set of rules and its own fine lines of distinction; it is hard to tell where cultural customs end and social delineations begin.

The situation is further complicated by the fact that certain class attributes in one culture may not be shared by the same class in another. For example, cleanliness (daily bathing) in the United States might be called a middle-class value, but it is not shared by the middle classes in some other countries. Making a scene in public is considered very low-class in England while in some others, it is seen as defending one's status. What is considered decent dress or courteous behavior by a certain class in one culture may or may not hold for the same class in another. Unfortunately the foreigner may never know for sure.

Class difference, when it is present, is one of the major causes of conflict in intercultural marriage, as in any marriage, because it carries over into so many other areas. The way people blow their nose, chew their food, sit or stand in public, or interact with peers has as much to do with family, educational, and social background as it does with nationality. These class-determined behaviors are the very fabric of daily life. Social background will determine not only the behavior of the spouse but also the attitude toward many other things that will be a part of their life together: sex, educational goals, work, recreation, financial management, leisure activities, role definitions, and so on.

Although class difference is one of the major issues in an intercultural marriage, it is often overlooked as a culprit when things begin to go wrong; usually the cultural differences get blamed instead. "She does this or that because of her Polish/Moroccan/English, etc., background." In a roundabout way this is true—the cultural difference is to blame, probably because the couple made the error of marrying across class *because* they were foreign to one another and didn't perceive the class differences. In one's own culture, one just knows, but gaining that kind of knowledge can take a long time in another culture, and by that time they often are already married.

14

Religion

Believing where we cannot prove.
—Tennyson, *In Memoriam*

Between couples from the same country, different religious beliefs can be a cause of conflict in marriage, not only because the partners may not be in agreement on where and how to worship as a family, but because so much of what people do and believe, their attitudes about what is right and wrong, and their philosophy of life stem from their religious background.

In any marriage, problems can arise when religious beliefs differ or when one partner's behavior conflicts with the other's beliefs. Mutual respect for each other's religion is a must for a compatible marriage, but often it is not enough. "Live and let live" doesn't work for everyone.

Some religions deny the validity of all others and insist on conversion or demand that the children be brought up in that religion. Orthodox Judaism, for example, teaches that the family must repudiate (sit *shive* for) a child who marries a non-Jew; Islam demands obedience to God's law only as revealed by Muhammad and also requires that a Muslim woman marry a fellow Muslim. The Catholic Church until recent years insisted that a non-Catholic partner sign a prenuptial agreement to raise any children Catholic.

In other cases people enter intercultural marriages only to find that difference of religion is a life-encompassing issue because they live in a country where the dictates of religion determine or strongly influence accepted behavior. Frequently it is difficult to know where religion ends and cultural values begin. The problem is aggravated if one partner is intensely religious and the other less so. Even people who do not actively practice their religion are often influenced by the values and thought patterns of their religious past. Sometimes couples think they have resolved the religion issue because they have settled on where to marry and in what kind of ceremony and have come to some sort of agreement regarding where to worship and how to raise the children. But religion runs deeper than that and can well up disruptively if not carefully attended to.

In Muslim countries it is religion which determines the degree of freedom women have; it regulates such things as gambling, dancing, sexual behavior, and the use of alcohol. In Latin American countries the Catholic Church, with its veneration of the Virgin Mary, is behind many of the prevailing attitudes toward women, judging them according to their approximation to her as virgins and mothers. In India the Hindu way of life, with its division of people into castes and its concept of *dharma* (system of conduct), regulates behavior. In the United States, where there are numerous religions, much of what is considered proper behavior stems from Puritan–Protestant origins.

For those couples who decide to override the dictates of their religions and marry outside them (often in the face of parental or community interference or withdrawal of support), one of three things usually happens: (1) one partner converts to the religion of the other; (2) both partners keep their own faith and try not to interfere in the practices or beliefs of the other; or (3) both partners drift away from their own religion and either join a third religion or refrain from adhering to any formal religion at all. In many cases both of the spouses have already distanced themselves from their cultural heritage, and religious practice is not an issue.[1]

---

[1] A comparative study of intermarriage in Northern Ireland (Catholic-Protestant) and in Pakistan (Muslims with Christians or Hindus) found that in Ireland the man who marries out of his religion is considered lost because the women are seen as the keepers of the faith. In Pakistan, however, it is the opposite: women are considered to be morally weaker than men, and so it is more serious for a woman to marry a non-Muslim than for a man. Donnan, "Mixed Marriage in Comparative Perspective," 208–25.

Adela, a nonpracticing Cuban Catholic, was fascinated by Mohammed's Muslim faith, and because of its rigidity, she thought it would be easier for everyone if she converted. There were many things she had difficulty accepting but, under Mohammed's instructions, she tried her best to conform to the laws of the Prophet.

In contrast, Daniele, living in Morocco, could not bring herself to abandon her Catholic faith, even if she did not actively practice it. Although her husband, Mehdi, tried to convince her, explaining that if she did not convert, under the law (especially as a foreign wife) she stood to lose her inheritance and perhaps even the guardianship of her children if anything were to happen to him. Still, she felt it would be hypocritical to convert without belief, and Mehdi respected her decision.

Kimberly, a self-styled American "super-Jew" and her Cambodian Buddhist husband, Louis, both felt strongly about their own religion and chose a system of noninterference in each other's beliefs. However, they found that they both actively practiced their faith less and regretted not being able to share it with each other.

Massimo and Tove were without strong bonds to their own religion and, like many couples, raised their children without any formal religion whatsoever. Since the two found all religions equal and interesting, when they felt the need for collective prayer, they would go to the church or the temple of the country to which they were currently assigned. When they were in Italy with Massimo's Catholic family, they would go to Mass with them; when in Denmark, they would keep Tove's family happy by attending Lutheran services.

But this kind of solution is not possible for everyone because to many people, the form of their relationship to God is an all-important matter. One Indian Hindu, who turned his back on his faith and his family to marry a Christian foreigner, was never able to make peace with his own conscience. For most of the couple's life together he was subject to nervous disorders, which he blamed on his religious and cultural desertion. He not only suffered feelings of guilt for his decision but also later on came to resent his wife for having influenced his choice.

Most couples confront the religious issue before they marry and reach some sort of compromise or agreement. In many cases, however, they can't really identify or explain to the other just what their religion means to them, because it isn't something they have ever verbalized. They often don't get to the issues which later will cause disagreement or misunderstanding in their daily lives. As one Italian psychologist explains it, in religion as in culture, we often don't know where our feet end until someone steps on our toes.

As regards the formal practice of religion, the agreement often works; few couples have arguments regarding theology. But religious beliefs resurface in many forms and frequently determine how a couple's life together will be played out: how many children a couple will have, the use of birth control, attitude toward abortion, fidelity, divorce; whether family funds will be donated to religious institutions; how holidays will be spent (how much time will be devoted to religious ceremonies and celebrations and which will be observed in the home); which food will be served in the house; how one or both will dress or behave in various circumstances; what moral code, medical practices, and so on, they will adhere to.

Adela found that converting to Islam was not a simple matter of changing her place of worship; it meant, especially for a woman, accepting a totally different style of life. Her Iranian husband, Mohammed, not only abhorred what he considered overt sexuality on television, he expected her to repudiate it as well and to stop watching some of her favorite programs because they contained immoral scenes. She had to change her way of dressing, which meant avoiding makeup, wearing clothes with sleeves, and giving up days at the beach so dear to her Cuban heart, because he could not permit his wife to be seen scantily clad by other men. She had to restrain her natural exuberance with old friends, offering the men a staid handshake in place of a friendly hug, which caused her friends to wonder why she had turned so cold.

Buddhist Louis and Jewish Kimberly found that their marriage was enriched by the philosophies and traditions of their respective religions and in the beginning took turns participating in one another's ceremonies with solemn respect. Kimberly even tried meditating with Louis every morning before both left for work. All went well except for one minor problem: Louis hated Jewish food—gefilte fish, chopped liver, and lox. Every Jewish holiday was a torture for him, and rather than offend anyone by saying so, he began to boycott holidays with her family, thus causing arguments with his wife and hard feelings between him and his in-laws. Only when they had been married for a few years did the truth come out and all was forgiven; it became a family joke.

Couples with the same religion, but who come from different lands, often find differences in their interpretation of the doctrines and laws of their faith. Latin and Irish Catholics, for example, see things like church attendance and immorality differently; the former emphasizes the loving church and the other, the authoritarian one. Mario and Deirdre found, for example, that while both believed in the same sins, one felt guiltier than the other about committing them. Sometimes partners of the same religion not only disagree but are shocked by the other's interpretation of the religious laws. Iranian and Egyptian Muslims often see things quite differently (and react differently to the wave of fundamentalism flowing through their countries), as do many American and Israeli Jews. Many African Christians combine Christianity with tribal beliefs, practices, and rituals.

Even when agreements have been made and religious compromises worked out as circumstances change, these accords may no longer function and have to be reworked.

Yvette found that when she and Ali moved to Kuwait, their agreement to "live and let live" was assaulted from all sides. He was under pressure from his family to force her to convert, or at least to conform; she felt trapped and detested the restrictions placed on her by the society at large.

Mehdi, in order to protect Daniele under the law, named his best friend (also married to a foreign woman) as his children's guardian in the event that something happened to him. Daniele agreed that the children would be raised Muslim as long as they were also exposed to her Christian faith. It turned out that the children, while they felt culturally Muslim, were actually more attracted to the Christian faith, something neither of them could have predicted.

When children arrive, buried beliefs resurface. Sometimes adults who had stopped practicing their religion return to the fold as parents, feeling the need to impart their beliefs or moral code to their offspring. Although a couple may have decided beforehand on the child's religion, one partner may only give lip service to the decision or may boycott it in subtle (or obvious) ways, showing through actions a lack of adherence to or even respect for the other's teachings. Deirdre, for example, complained, "It is hard to instill religious beliefs or values all alone when the child sees the other parent doing otherwise. Inevitably the child will choose the easier route."

Many intercultural couples have thanked God that they have the bond of a common religion to help them overcome problems their other differences have caused. Others feel that a common religion is not as important as the strength of their inner beliefs and personal moral code. It is the degree of their devoutness or spirituality which matters, whatever their religious affiliation. What is important is that the partners become aware of and able to articulate the beliefs and discuss the practices which are most important in their religious heritage. Without this, successful negotiation on religious matters is unlikely to occur.

15

Raising Children

> I try to discourage mixed marriages…[but] they'll be okay as long as they can stay sterile [childless]. Once they have children, they have a problem.
> —Rabbi Stanley Rabinowitz, quoted by Janet Wallach
> *Washington Post Magazine,* 11 November 1984

> Evolution works by mixing bloodlines so that there will always be someone around who can adapt to change. Variety is not just the spice of life, it's evolution's crucial ingredient.
> —Diane Ackerman
> *A Natural History of Love,* 1994

"We were fine until the children came along" is a familiar refrain among many intercultural couples. Even when everything else is smooth sailing, disagreements over how best to raise the children often make the going rough. Obviously the job is easier for those who come from similar backgrounds and who agree on the details of how to discipline, guide, and nurture their children, but many intercultural couples don't have that luxury. Furthermore, they worry not only about the day-to-day logistics of bringing up their children but also about the psychological impact of their being bicultural and sometimes biracial, the whole identity issue. Raising children is an important issue for each parent, and each is genuinely concerned that the best thing possible be done for the children. Too often, though, what each sees as best is what each has known and been taught; past experience is what will generally be repeated. Usually without analyzing what they are doing, most people automatically revert to their own childhood to find a model for parenting, for teaching survival skills and the unspoken conventions of relationships. Because they were raised in different countries and cultures, the parents may have not only different but also conflicting models. Parents may find themselves at odds in agreeing upon a clear and consistent pattern for their children. Parents in basic agreement regarding their value system may still find that they emphasize different values while raising their children. The desired end result might be the same, but the route along the way might differ radically.

Parents who clash over child-rearing issues are often really battling over some basic difference in philosophy, values, or beliefs that they as a couple have not managed to resolve; the child merely provides the spark for conflict. But these underlying issues are often difficult to recognize or define, let alone come to grips with; so, instead of going to the heart of the matter, the couple fights over the particulars.

Often differences show up before the child is born. What religion and what language should be taught? Should family celebrations reflect both cultures and both religions (as a means of keeping the child connected) or should the host country win out? Should the child be raised monocultural or bicultural, monolingual or bilingual? Are the parents prepared, especially in a biracial marriage, for the fact that the child may be a blend and not look like either parent? Are the grandparents prepared that the child might look and be completely different from "their side"?

Choosing the name can be a cause of discord: Should it be a family name, and if so, whose family? Should the name be typical of one culture, one country, one religion, or should it be one which is acceptable to both?[1]

---

[1] "...in France, everyone, irrespective of religion or national origin, has to choose first names for their French-born children that are taken from a government list of French names of Catholic saints...." H. Ned Seelye and Jacqueline H. Wasilewski, *Between Cultures: Developing Self-Identity in a World of Diversity* (Lincolnwood, IL: National Textbook, 1996), 14.

There are different ideas about how infants should be handled. Should the baby sleep on its side or on a pile of pillows, with a wool or cotton undershirt, in a room with closed or open windows, alone or with the parents? Should it be breast- or bottle-fed, on schedule or on demand? Should its every cry be answered or should it be trained to control itself? Should it be allowed to crawl on the floor, walk barefoot, stumble and fall, or be pampered and protected from potential dangers before they present themselves? Should a doctor be called at every variation of temperature? Should child care be the exclusive domain of the mother, shared by both parents, or entrusted to a nursemaid or relatives?

In childhood there are problems of schooling and training. Should boys and girls be educated equally? Together or separately? Should first sons be given preferential treatment? Is aggressiveness between siblings a preparation for the struggle ahead in life or an antisocial act? Is rebelliousness a sign of disrespect toward elders or a healthy progression toward independence? Should the schooling be done in one or both languages, one or both cultural systems? Should the child go to school alone or be accompanied by a parent? Should parents be actively involved in the child's schoolwork, monitoring every step, or should the child be responsible for his or her own work and the consequences of not doing it well? Does performing poorly at school bring shame on the entire family or on the child alone?

In early adulthood there are questions regarding how much and when to let go of the child, questions regarding sexuality, freedom, and filial duty and respect. Should a girl go out alone? Should children choose their own friends, their own mates, live on their own as young adults, or with their parents until they marry? Should they earn their own spending money and be responsible for chores around the house, or should they be given an allowance until they are out on their own? The answers to these questions depend a great deal on the cultures involved.

As if it's not enough for the parents themselves to have to come to some agreement regarding these matters, the extended families (the new grandparents, uncles, aunts) often take an active role and offer advice, comments, and criticism (solicited or not). Sometimes they actually interfere, occasionally showing preference or support for the child who is more like them, which makes the parents' job harder.

Most of the potential disagreements mentioned above arise over details, details which are surface manifestations of deeply held beliefs, values, and traditions. For the sake of simplicity we can classify most of the issues into one of three categories: (1) values and beliefs, (2) educational and disciplinary styles, and (3) forms of relationship between parent and child.

Values and Beliefs

As we discussed earlier, values and beliefs define who we are, what is true, and what is right and wrong, the "musts" and "must nots." They are first learned at home and then often vanish into our subconscious until something causes them to surface, something which challenges them. Many fortunate couples discover that, despite their many other differences, their basic beliefs and values are the same, and they are able, each in his or her own way, to instill the same strong personal code in their children. Other couples clash. Some clash only in private, others in front of the children. When the parents' values are not only different but also conflicting, there is bound to be trouble for both parents and children. Because so few people are able to stand back and analyze their beliefs and behaviors, the conflict is hard to understand and the clashes can be difficult to resolve. One or the other might compromise but feel a sense of loss or of failure for not being able to pass along deeply felt beliefs or values. One may feel alienated from his or her children if they adopt the standards of the other parent's culture. The children themselves often feel confused by the lack of clarity and consistency in the messages they receive from their parents. In the worst-case scenario some are rewarded by one parent and punished by the other for the same behavior.

Children whose parents are involved in a values tug-of-war may choose the values of the more lenient parent; others, forced to choose those of the more dominant parent, may give lip service to them but underneath it all remain confused or unsure. Some, whose parents expose them to (but do not fight over) contradictory standards, benefit from the double exposure and, having had to work things through for themselves, actually are stronger as a result. Needless to say, the socialization process does not depend on the parents alone; children are influenced by the other adults they encounter during their lives (relatives, teachers, parents of friends, religious figures, coaches, etc.) as well as by their own peers, and so the place where they live will play a big part.

Jaime and Cassie fought frequently over their daughter, Jennifer. Many of their unresolved conflicts stemmed from differences in values, which came into play when there were decisions to be made regarding Jennifer. As a baby, should she be allowed to play on the beach without any clothes; as a child, to roughhouse in faded jeans or be required to play in freshly ironed dresses; as a teen, to choose her own friends and dates? The arguments were endless. They bickered at every stage of her growth over what appeared to be details, but details which reflected their culturally different values regarding male–female roles, virtue, good manners, and so on.

Jennifer waited each time to see who would win. She waited in vain to receive one absolute and permanent answer which would tell her what was right and what was wrong. She felt torn apart by her parents' differences, was unable to obey one without turning against the other, and finally learned to play one against the other to achieve her own goals. As time went on, Jennifer became more confused and unsure of herself, indecisive, and, at the same time, rebellious against any and all authority. With each battle Cassie and Jaime grew further apart. They blamed each other for everything that went wrong with the child but never faced the fact that it was their unresolved value conflicts which were causing their child-rearing disagreements.

Frequently, couples claim the same values but define them differently. Fiamma, the flamboyant Italian, and her English husband, Andrew, both taught their children to be honest, but their culturally guided interpretations of dishonesty were different. Paying bribes and avoiding taxes were a way of life for Fiamma, but for Andrew they were forms of cheating. While both claimed the same value, their children heard conflicting messages.

Culturally different values do not always mean conflicting values, and many children of bicultural parents have benefited from the exposure to both systems. Massimo's wife, Tove (one of whose parents had been Danish and the other Egyptian), described herself as diluted because of her two cultures and felt that she was more tolerant, more broad-minded than most of her contemporaries.

> I learned at an early age to listen to two sides of every question and to think things through, not just automatically accept what I was told. My parents let me know that there were different ways of seeing things, that they didn't always agree, but that was all right. I guess it depends on how the differences are presented to the kids—as problems or as distinctions. As a result I believe I am more open and accepting of new ideas, new ways, different beliefs. But then again, I am also strongly attached to none: maybe that's good, maybe not.

Educational and Disciplinary Styles

Parents' educational and disciplinary styles depend a great deal on their value systems: on how they perceive their role in life and their relations with others and on their perception of the world and themselves. In other words, how they will instruct their children to behave will depend in part on whether their orientation is toward *doing* or *being*; on whether they believe in the equality of all people or in a hierarchical system; and on whether they see themselves primarily as individuals, and therefore responsible for their own future, or as an integral part of a group.

With the intercultural couple, as we have seen, these value systems are sometimes the same, sometimes not—which also means that sometimes their educational methods are the same and sometimes not.

Some cultures (Latin American, Asian, Middle Eastern, and many European) adhere to more authoritarian methods based on patriarchal systems, while others (American, Anglo, Scandinavian, Polynesian, etc.) are generally more lenient and permissive. This usually means that in the authoritarian family, the parental word is final and there is little room for negotiation; the child must obey. In the permissive family, children are encouraged to participate in the decision making, express opinions and ideas, ask "why," and at least make an attempt to negotiate with the parents. These two orientations make for very different family dynamics and can be the cause of intense conflict when couples come from opposite sides of the fence.

"French and Americans," says Raymonde Carroll in *Cultural Misunderstandings*, "seem to be in agreement on only one point: they do not understand (which means they do not approve of) the way in which the children of the 'other culture' are raised."[2]

One of the most frequent child-related problems encountered in these marriages revolves around differences regarding punishment of the errant child, specifically the kinds of punishment and the amount.

Yvette, for example, had no problem with Ali's authoritarian orientation; her own upbringing had been a strict, patriarchal one, but she put her foot down at the harsh physical punishment Ali considered right and necessary to enforce his authority. Quick-tempered, he demanded unquestioning obedience and responded to any lack of it with his hands, pulling the children into submission by their hair, slapping any rebelliousness out of them and, on one or two unforgettable occasions, kicking them into silence. Not a cruel man, he merely practiced what he knew, what he believed was the best way to teach them proper behavior. But it was treatment Yvette could not bear to witness in silence as the other women of his culture did. Inevitably she interfered, only increasing his anger and, in the long run, causing him to do more physical harm to the children. As they grew older they pleaded with her not to interfere: "It only makes him get worse," they begged her.

This disagreement caused more conflict than anything else in their marriage. Ali maintained that Yvette was undermining his authority and that their children would be the worse for it; she felt she had to compensate for his undue severity though it meant being more lenient with them than she, by nature, would have chosen to be. She struggled with the dilemma: would everyone be better off if she just accepted Ali's methods, or was it her duty to participate actively in disciplining the children? All she knew was that she wasn't comfortable with Ali's methods and that her children would grow away from her if she did not remain true to herself and get involved.

---

[2] Carroll, *Cultural Misunderstandings*, 41.

Kimberly and Louis had a similar problem. He was dismayed that she yelled at and boxed their children's ears, although he knew that she was as quick to hug as to hit. Still, for him it was too physical, too loud, and too emotional. In protest he would leave the house during these scenes, causing her to claim that he wasn't helping.

Louis, however, believed in disciplining the children by withholding his love when he did not believe they merited it, which Kimberly found cold and psychologically damaging. He was especially severe with them when he felt they were being disrespectful by answering back or arguing against his decisions or when one of them (especially one of his sons) would shame him by crying in response to punishment. To Kimberly all of this was just healthy acting out. They never did agree, and both continued to handle the children in their own way. The children soon learned to expect different treatment from each parent—and to approach them in different ways.

Joachim and Sara had their biggest arguments over their children's manners, especially table manners, which were learned and enforced over what were (to Sara) painful meals. Sometimes she feared the children were being turned into little robots, though she had to admit she was glad she could count on their knowing how to behave in public, which saved her from being criticized. Joachim adhered very definitely to the philosophy that the children's behavior reflected on the parents' (i.e., mother's) parenting ability—so much so that Sara remembers the time she corrected her youngest son by saying, "What would your father say if I told him what you had done?" His astute reply drew her up short: "He'd say it was *your* fault."

Frequently differences in attitude toward child discipline will affect not only how the children are handled at home, but how their schooling is approached.

Lynn and Hans, who managed to carve out a life for themselves in their mountain village in Austria, waged a standing battle over the education of their son, Heinrich. Lynn, as a good American mother, was not only more lenient in her disciplinary methods, but believed as well that "learning should be fun" and resented the "parroting" method her son was being exposed to in the Austrian schools. She fought against it: she fought the teachers, the system, and her husband over the issue while Heinrich awaited the outcome. Hans maintained that the American way left children without *durchalten* (backbone), without a sense of the value of hard work and endurance, and without the automatic respect for authority figures which he considered essential to a child's formation. The teachers complained that Heinrich did not have the proper family support to be a good student (a mother who did his homework with him). Heinrich, caught in the middle, struggled to do his best amidst the confusion.

Cecil and Ikumi had differences of opinion regarding child rearing typical of East-West marriages—to which was added Cecil's adherence to the British belief in the benefits of boarding school. Although she recognized that sending their son back to England to be educated was better in some ways, considering the nomadic life they led in the foreign service, she never fully forgave him for insisting on doing so when the boy was only ten years of age.

Hiroshi and Dorrie had many similar problems. Dorrie criticized the Japanese school system as being stifling while Hiroshi pointed to the superior scholastic results. Dorrie strongly opposed the prevalent use of corporal punishment, while Hiroshi defended the rights of the teachers. "Truthfully," Dorrie confessed, "I have a problem with the whole system of raising and educating children in Japan. Hiroshi's interpretation of my role as a mother is in total contrast with my own. I didn't believe that I should sleep with the newborn while my husband got his rest down the hall, nor did I go along with breast-feeding until the child was two years old. It all goes with the Japanese view that the child is an extension of the mother. I see us as independent beings, which is alien and wrong to him."

Parent-Child Relationships

The disciplinary methods and the kind of family structure from which they derive—authoritarian or permissive—often strongly affect parent-child relationships: how parents show, and expect their children to show, love and respect. The authoritarian family follows a "rules over feelings" doctrine and the atmosphere is formal and respectful. Often the houses are set up to enforce this atmosphere, with parlors for adults only and formal dining rooms, where Papa presides and the children watch their manners and curb their tongues.

The permissive type of family is usually more casual, spontaneous, nurturing and more concerned with expressing feelings than
applying rules; it uses feedback and explains the reasons behind decisions. Houses usually reflect this style, revolving around the family
room, which is everyone's domain.[3]

When styles of interfamily relating are culturally different, couples
usually choose one of three courses. They may follow the customs of
the land. This usually means that the expatriate spouse adheres to
the at-home spouse's style. In some ways this is the easiest on the
child because there is consistency between how people act with one
another, both in and outside the home. Rashida did her best to be as
typical a Kenyan wife and mother as she could, so that her husband
and children would not be embarrassed by her in public. Her indoor
intimate relationship with her boys, however, was her own; it was
"our secret." Helga submerged herself in her husband's Libyan culture, speaking his language and adopting his manners, including the
way in which she related to their children. She felt that presenting a
united front would serve the children as role models in their future
relationships with others. But she found that this method, while advantageous in certain respects, involved a certain self-negation. When
she moved with the children to Geneva, she was able to revert to
German beliefs and behaviors, which was a relief to her but perplexing to the children.

The second possibility is to adopt the style of one partner, often
that of the more dominant one; or of the man in male-dominated
cultures; or sometimes that of the woman, when child rearing is considered her exclusive domain, regardless of where they are living.

In some cases, allowing one parent to dominate works; in others
it can be disastrous. For example, Adela submitted to her husband's
will and allowed him to create a strictly Muslim home, but their children were exposed to a totally different and appealing lifestyle in the
Philadelphia public schools they attended. In their case the conflict of
lifestyles became too much for their youngest daughter, Jasmine, who
fled from home at age sixteen, at least in part to escape the ambiva-

---

[3] For more information on this subject see "Out of House and Home" in Condon
and Yousef, *An Introduction to Intercultural Communication*, 146–67.

lence of her life—a father who was so different from the people around them, a mother whom she saw as too weak to fight him, and friends who lived such different lives.

Milee and Harry educated their children in the Australian manner, sending them to local schools where they spoke English, played Australian sports, and joined in a variety of extracurricular activities. However, when they entered their home, the children were expected by their mother and Vietnamese resident relatives to become perfect Asian children, deferring to the adult family's wishes without argument, eating Vietnamese food, and controlling any Western impulses they may have picked up on the outside. At the same time, because Harry's work took him out of town frequently and no one else was totally fluent in English, their eldest daughter took on many extra responsibilities for the family: interpreting for her mother, helping the younger children with their homework, fielding business phone calls, dealing with officials, and so on. On one hand, she had to be the adult in the house and become mature far beyond her years, but on the other hand, show childlike deference to all the resident elders. Harry had some trouble with this pattern but felt his hands were tied because of the constant presence of Milee's family and because he was away too much on assignment around the country to exert much influence.

The third alternative is for both parents to behave individually in their own natural and comfortable way with their children. This usually happens when both partners are from fairly egalitarian cultures, when both are considered equal partners in the marriage, and when each respects the other. This was the case with Massimo and Tove because both partners liked and admired the other's culture, felt that each parent had something special to offer, and did not interfere with how each worked out his or her personal relationship with the children. Not that they always agreed, but they learned how important it was to give the other partner space and autonomy to handle their children in his or her own way.

Duncan and Eva divided their parental roles: Eva handled the daily problems and Duncan the long-term ones. Eva was more on top of the children's concerns or infractions and dealt with them decisively. Duncan, who was much more inclined to "let the kids get out of their own mess," entered the picture only when required. In time, the children learned that their best bet was to get to their father first, as he was usually more lenient with them than their strict German mother.

Their real challenge as parents came when Duncan's children from his first marriage came to live with them after their mother died. Not only did they resent their stepmother in principle but they bristled under the new "home rules" to which they were being subjected. Eva's and their American mother's ideas regarding neatness, comportment, and discipline couldn't have been more different, and the children contested every correction as a criticism of their mother. This stressful situation tested the solidity of the relationship between Duncan and Eva and caused their own children to begin to question many things they had taken for granted. It was not an easy time for anyone and called for more involvement on the part of Duncan, who found himself having to cross cultures within his own family.

The primary disadvantage for children of parents who each relate and show love to them in different ways is that the children have not had a hard and fast role model for how to relate or show love to their own peers or to other adults. Some believe that these children become more withdrawn or shy because they don't have a clear and instinctive sense of how to act. But others benefit from the double example; they learn at an early age how to get along with all kinds of people and become effective communicators who are more alert to signals and nonverbal messages than others. They can sense more quickly what people expect and see details others don't see, though at the risk, as one bicultural individual put it, of "seeing or understanding neither culture completely because I haven't grown up totally in either." But for many it is just part of growing up. As one explained, "For my sister and me, being bicultural is as natural as being monocultural is to our friends. We didn't realize we were different till we went to school. I really don't think we have any *more* psychological problems than our monocultural friends, we just have different ones."

Two of the biggest issues faced by concerned intercultural parents revolve around questions of the "identity" of the bicultural child and of bilingualism.

Many worry that the children will have problems if they are not given firm roots in a single culture. This usually means immersion in the country in which they live, resulting in a monocultural upbringing—at home, at school, and in the language used. This denies the children access to their mixed heritage, which the children often ultimately resent. Lynn and Hans's son knew nothing of his mother's culture because she threw herself completely into becoming a model Austrian woman herself and, except for the battles with the schools, chose to let the Austrian culture and language dominate totally in their home. Only later did she realize that by so doing she was alienating Heinrich not only from part of his cultural heritage but from herself as well. At that point she decided to arrange for him to spend extended periods of time in the States, but "by then," Heinrich said, "it was almost too late; I went to America as a foreigner."

Others maintain that "only trees need roots" and that their children benefit from exposure to multiple cultures and languages and an international atmosphere. Some believe that because of their mixed heritage their children are on the cutting edge of what will be the way of life in the twenty-first century. "Our kids, because of their mixed heritage and global lifestyle, are not only bicultural but multicultural. They have so much less to unlearn than monocultural people that they can move automatically into different mindsets, different frameworks."

However, the children of these couples will usually tell you that some connectedness is important. One self-described "international" woman who was the offspring of an American mother and Chinese father but raised in Rome and sent to British schools after her mother and father divorced, felt cheated of her heritage. First, she had no contact with the culture of her father except for the physical characteristics of his race: "I have a face that identifies me with a culture I don't know." Second, she never spent more than a few months at a time in the land of her mother: "I have an American passport,...speak English with a British accent, and have Italian friends. Wherever I am, I feel like an impostor. Thank heavens my (Lebanese) husband himself had a nomadic upbringing so he can at least understand me. But I envy people who have some culture they can cling to."

As pointed out by Seelye and Wasilewski in *Between Cultures*, "Some multicultural people who may feel at home in many places actually resolve the dilemma of an either/or choice by having *partial* identities that they use as appropriate, depending on the social context."[4] Fiona, the daughter of Irish Deirdre and Italian Mario, related that she doesn't "feel Italian or Irish or American or Argentinian" (referring to places where she spent some of her growing-up years). "I am a chameleon. When I was younger, that bothered me, but now I rather enjoy my fuzziness. I confuse people. I like that. It amuses me that they can't pigeonhole me. I am foreign. There are advantages, you know, to being the foreigner (but one who knows the ropes) wherever you go; you can get away with more."

But obviously not all bicultural children feel that their double heritage is as much of a blessing as it is a burden. Bicultural and, especially, biracial kids frequently have major identity problems. In the United States children of a racially mixed black and white marriage are publicly pressured to be black, no matter how they feel about themselves or how much that may mean having to deny the white parent. This caused Bill and Mary's (American/Nigerian) daughter to develop a private and a public persona. In a study of mixed black and white young adults it was found that "...society's insistence that interracial children are simply black...undermines the formation of a healthy racial identity and creates conflicts." It found that the most frequently utilized coping mechanism, and the one associated with the least inner conflict, was that of a public black identity and a private interracial one.[5]

Dorrie and Hiroshi's son, born and raised in Japan but with the coloring of his Dutch mother, described himself as "an undercover Japanese. I look like a *gaijin* (foreigner) but I have the soul of a Japanese."

Another young man, born Palestinian with a Jordanian passport, the son of a Muslim father and a German–Jewish mother, was torn between the hatred and anger which divided Arabs and Jews and his own mixed feelings about understanding and accepting both of them. He felt that his only hope was to "leave Jerusalem, which is where I

---

[4] Seelye and Wasilewski, *Between Cultures*, 103.
[5] Ursula M. Brown, "Black/White Interracial Young Adults: Quest for a Racial Identity," *American Journal of Orthopsychiatrics* 65, no. 1 (January 1995): 125.

studied and where I want to live, and go to Europe or America, where I have some chance at having a life."

Many parents rightly worry about having children who will be "marginal," or "on the margin of each culture, but a member of neither."[6] They worry that they may be handicapping their children at the same time as they are giving them a multiple heritage and wonder whether this is a gift or a curse. They fear that they might possibly be raising children who will suffer from what Seelye and Wasilewski call "authenticity anxiety." "If they use language and behavior so that they 'play' well in different cultural contexts, are they being their true selves? Are they being sincere?"[7] It is a legitimate concern, and one that has been studied by cross-cultural trainer and researcher Janet M. Bennett. She makes a distinction between what she calls *encapsulated marginality* and *constructive marginality*. By encapsulated marginality, she means a person who is "buffeted by conflicting cultural loyalties and unable to construct a unified identity." Constructive marginality refers to a person who is "able to construct context intentionally and consciously for the purpose of creating his or her own identity."[8] Most children of intercultural marriages will tell you that, while during adolescence they fit more into the encapsulated category and were confused and perhaps even distressed, as adults they have found and rather like themselves in their biculturality. As Rosemary and Ravi's son, who was half American and half Indian, explained it, "You eventually make up your own identity out of your own life."

Most of the parents who have seen their children through the difficult adolescent years, when being different is devastating, believe that in the long run their children benefit from full exposure to all their cultures. The important thing seems to be to give them a positive sense of their dual or multicultural heritage so that they are strong and comfortable with it, so that instead of feeling they are half some-

---

[6] Milton M. Goldberg, "A Qualification of the Marginal Man Theory," *American Sociological Review* 6 (1941): 58.

[7] Seelye and Wasilewski, *Between Cultures*, 94.

[8] Janet M. Bennett, "Cultural Marginality: Identity Issues in Intercultural Training," in *Education for the Intercultural Experience*, edited by R. Michael Paige (Yarmouth, ME: Intercultural Press, 1993), 113.

thing, they feel they are double something. The secret appears to lie in the parents' ability to encourage open discussion of the children's mixed heritage as well as in the opportunity given the children to develop positive relationships with both cultural or racial groups. A parent who denigrates the other parent's culture with comments showing disapproval of certain cultural characteristics which the children might be adopting will give negative messages regarding the desirability of being part of that other culture. Obviously, this is far less likely to happen if the parents themselves respect and honestly promote one another's cultural background.

The parents' esteem for each other's culture can be expressed in their interest in and/or willingness to study the other's language, which, of course, opens the door to helping the children learn it too. If parents don't learn their spouse's language, then helping the children learn it will be more difficult. As Alvino Fantini of the School for International Training has pointed out, language serves to communicate but also to excommunicate; it excludes those who don't understand.[9] Thus one parent's willingness to study the language of the other validates that other language for the children, encouraging them to become bilingual.

Many parents, however, are against bringing their children up in more than one language for fear that it will handicap them. This fear was reinforced by researchers in the first half of the twentieth century, who believed that bilingualism adversely affected children's intelligence. More recent experiments in bilingualism, which have been carried out in several U.S. school systems (Portland, Oregon and Anchorage, Alaska, among others), have shown that, quite the contrary, learning another language opens new pathways of connections in the brain as well as helping the children become more flexible in their analytical and critical thinking. However, "Bilingual children," Seelye and Wasilewski tell us, "do tend to have a lower vocabulary in either of their languages than that possessed by their monolingual peers.... Different reasons are offered to explain this. For one, the child tends

---

[9]   Alvino Fantini, ed., "Introduction—Language, Culture and Worldview: Explaining the Nexus," *International Journal of Intercultural Relations* 19, no. 2 (Spring 1995): 148.

to hear each language less since time is shared between two (or more) languages."[10]

Yet, being bilingual is one of the advantages most often cited by bicultural children. Many remember complaining about having to learn the second language, being embarrassed as children if a parent spoke the "other" language in public, and refusing to answer in one parent's language as an act of spite when angry at that parent, but in the end being grateful for the advantage it gave them. Knowing the language of a culture gives access to that culture. For these bicultural children it means access to part of their heritage, which most of them feel is their right. No matter what the method of instilling the second language, clarity and consistency, according to linguist Fantini, are the two most important ingredients. But also try to make the experience enjoyable. Forcing it on an unwilling child can backfire. The whole process is easier if children can be made to see that knowing the language will in both the short and the long run be advantageous to them.

Raising children is the real test of how well a couple has learned to handle their many differences; with children all the issues surface and must be confronted. Differences don't matter. How they are managed does.

---

[10] Seelye and Wasilewski, *Between Cultures*, 51.

16

Language and Communication

I tried to say I love you, but the words got in the way.
          —*Miami Sound Machine*, Epic Records (CBS, Inc.)

A different language is a different vision of life.
                              —Federico Fellini

At the beginning of an intercultural couple's relationship, good communication is rarely seen as a major problem because each of the partners puts a lot of time and effort into understanding and being understood. Without realizing what they are doing, they continually question, explain, and clarify their meanings to each other. But at the same time, each takes for granted that his or her way of communicating is universal, obvious, clear, and right; they each assume that the other means what they themselves would mean if they said the same thing in the same way.[1] Only later do they begin to see that this is not true, and they begin to wonder whether they understand each other at all.

Communication is sharing meaning and includes everything we use to exchange meaning with one another: words, tone of voice, a shoulder shrug, a yawn, silence. It is hard enough for us in our own language to express our thoughts and feelings, to be understood, and to be sure we really understand others. When we try to communicate with a spouse (perhaps in his or her language) from a different linguistic and cultural background (as well as of the opposite sex—a cultural difference in itself), it becomes especially difficult.

---

[1] See Deborah Tannen, *That's Not What I Meant* (New York: Ballantine Books, 1986), 27.

Good communication is perhaps the most essential ingredient in a successful marriage, and it is probably the most difficult to achieve. Even in a monocultural marriage it is hard to express deeply felt fears, insecurities, desires, hopes, and regrets and to relate past events (especially painful ones). In an intercultural one, it is just that much harder, not only because the words may not come easily or accurately as a result of linguistic differences, but because of fear that the partner may not understand what is said and/or will interpret or judge it negatively from a culturally different perspective. How a couple shares meaning, how they decode each other's words and signs, pretty much determines the kind of relationship they will have.

Researchers have found that the "average person spends 50 to 80 percent of his day listening, but hears only half of what is said, understands only a quarter of that, and remembers even less."[2] In our own language we tune out, half-listen, become distracted, or are busy preparing our answers instead of really hearing. If listening is inherently such a difficult task, it is no wonder that intercultural couples have such a struggle with it.

Man Keung Ho, in *Building a Successful Intermarriage*, makes use of the Chinese word *ting* (listen) to explain its complexity. Ting is a composite of four vital parts.

---

2 Don Oldenburg, "In One Ear...," *Washington Post*, 27 February 1987, C5.

The ear is necessary for hearing the words spoken; the eye, for seeing the message conveyed by the body; the mind, for interpreting the meaning of what has been seen and heard; and the heart, for being able to feel what is wanted and needed from the relationship.[3]

In order for intercultural couples to overcome their communication handicaps, they have to work harder at listening, using the heart and mind as well as the eye and ear to avoid misunderstandings.

Other obstacles also block communication. Usually one of the two is not speaking his or her own language, which means that the message is possibly distorted by the foreign speaker and possibly only partially understood by the listener. Then, the message sent and received is subject to each listener's interpretation, which depends on his or her own personal and cultural frame of reference (including not only such things as differing conversational cues and style, but also expectations, gender bias, insecurities, wants, values, beliefs, prejudices). With such stumbling blocks, it's a wonder anything is communicated at all! But it is; it just takes a lot of hard work and patience.

In trying to unravel some of the mysteries of communication, it may help to examine its three major components—verbal, nonverbal, and stylistic. All three together can cause major problems for two people who do not come from the same linguistic and cultural background but who are trying to achieve an intimate relationship. Sometimes it takes years of practice as well as humor and a willingness to delve into hidden meanings for these couples to learn how to communicate with each other. This doesn't mean that the differences will go away but that spouses can learn to account for and adjust to them.

Verbal Communication

Verbal communication refers to the words we speak; it transmits the sense of what we want to say. At best, however, words are imperfect communicators, and for people who don't have the same mother

---

[3] Man Keung Ho, *Building a Successful Intermarriage between Religions, Social Classes, Ethnic Groups or Races* (St. Meinrad, IN: St. Meinrad Archabbey, 1984), 98.

tongue, they can be dangerous. It is not always easy in another language to know what words should be used when or to whom. Different rules apply in different cultures, and a wrong or inappropriate word can cause misunderstandings. A harmless expletive in one language (or the use of an expletive by a woman), translated literally into another, can be shocking or wounding; a *you* instead of a *thou* in some languages (French and German) can imply a familiarity which is not intended or proper.

All languages are made up of idiomatic phrases, figures of speech, and titles which convey certain meanings without elaborating. But these can be dangerous or disconcerting for someone with a different mother tongue. For example, saying to someone learning English, "hit the road" or "get a life," calls up confusing messages.

Titles, for example, are basically job descriptions—they describe the person who does this or that. But as many couples have found, certain titles carry different cultural interpretations. *Mother*, to Rosemary, for example, was the nurturer who led her children into adulthood and then let them go. To her Indian mother-in-law, however, *Mother* was the eternal presence in the lives of her children, dictating their lifestyle and demanding overt demonstrations of their loyalty.

In addition to the words themselves, language often affects the balance of power in an intercultural marriage. Generally one partner is speaking his or her own language and the other is not (except where both speak the same mother tongue or a third language); and because language is power, the more fluent partner has the upper hand and usually takes the lead. The spouse with superior linguistic facility, speed, and vocabulary can not only direct the conversation and set its style but also manipulate it to serve personal ends. And whenever this happens, the relationship suffers.[4]

Jaime, because of his limited knowledge of English, had to lean on Cassie for many things which he considered his male prerogative, and he resented it. Cassie, in turn, became impatient with Jaime's in-

---

[4] Some theories hold that the bilingual spouse has the advantage over the monolingual one as he or she "has already stretched his or her cognitive and affective powers...and is seen as more interculturally effective." Telser-Gadow, "Intercultural Communication Competence," 232.

effectiveness. She got tired of having to do everything "because no one else understands him." Despite her good intentions, she often became critical and bossy, which neither of them liked.

At the same time, Cassie made no attempt to learn Spanish. Basically she liked having the upper hand in this one important area. She liked the power that speaking in her own language gave her over a husband whose traditions taught him that women were slightly inferior beings. It was a small thing, but she hung on to it.

Both Cassie and Jaime commented on the fact that not having the same native language created tension in their daily lives, a tension which was draining. "Often we found that this tension…caused arguments which shouldn't have happened, which had nothing to do with the topic at the time. Because of the difficulties of communication, neither of us was relaxed; both of us were like bombs waiting to go off."

Lynn felt so strongly about not wanting to be helpless and dependent that she made a concerted effort to learn to speak and read German. In fact, she ended up speaking it better than Hans spoke English, and so it became their language of communication. But her sense of accomplishment waned when she had a difficult concept to explain, a deep feeling to express, or a point of view to defend. She would splutter hopelessly while Hans won out (right or wrong) through sheer verbal agility. Out of frustration she found that she often lashed out at him "like a viper" to compensate for her inadequacy with language.

Lynn also commented that she had "lost [her] personality in the translation, as well as [her] sense of humor." She felt she was leading a kind of double life, with one personality in one language, a second in the other, "…kind of an intercultural schizophrenic," as she put it. "In English I am a funny, clever woman; in German, I become a dummkopf. In fact the more I speak in German, the more I think I really am becoming dull. I miss the intellectual stimulation of conversing with people at the same level and in my own language, the repartee I had back home. We both have to watch so carefully not to misunderstand one another that it takes much of the fun out of talking."

It is often claimed that humor is the most difficult aspect of learning a language. Neither the words nor the concepts translate very well. Different cultures think different things are funny and make use of humor in their own way.

Milee often felt like crying—tears of frustration—because she was never able to see what was funny about Harry's jokes. His Australian friends admired his quick wit and wondered how he could have married someone so lacking in humor. But she knew how to laugh; she simply didn't understand her husband's jokes, even when they were painstakingly explained to her.

"I thought he was crazy," she said. "I thought they all were crazy. Then I tried laughing when the others were laughing but found that I was laughing at the wrong things and sometimes shocking everyone. Only Harry knew that I didn't understand, but when he explained to the others that I didn't know what I was laughing at, I felt even more ashamed and stupid. So we just gave up."

Deirdre, on the other hand, made use of wit when things "became so totally impossible that there was nothing else to do but laugh." She was also able to laugh at her own weaknesses and mistakes. Mario thought she needed to "have her head examined" to see how she could laugh "when she should have been crying." He also found her use of irony caustic, not funny. What he didn't understand was that laughing or making a wisecrack was her way of overcoming a desperate situation. She, in turn, thought that if he could forget *bella figura* and learn to take himself a little less seriously, it would be better for both of them.

Communication depends also on signals which the speaker gives (and the listener receives, interprets, and reacts to in his or her own way) through unspoken body language or nonverbal communication.

Nonverbal Communication

Just as the spoken language usually differs for couples from different cultural backgrounds, the nonverbal language is likely to be dissimilar as well. Whenever a person talks, *all* of that person is talking. Each of us makes use of a large set of nonverbal signals which convey meaning, sometimes more than the words themselves: tone of voice, intonation, facial gestures (grimaces, arched eyebrows, glancing heavenward, half-smiles, frowns), eye contact (either looking or not looking into another's eyes), body movements (drumming fingers, shrugging shoulders, waving arms), posture (slouching, poised, hunching forward), breathing patterns, and the distance maintained between speakers (intimately close or formally distant). These together form the framework for our spoken words and help send our message, and because these visible signals have been learned early in life, many are interpreted differently from culture to culture.

Many people are aware that nonverbal proficiency in a language really determines their fluency because this visible expressiveness often conveys information that is crucial to the understanding of the message. Unfortunately, it is difficult to learn because most nonverbal communication is unconscious, automatic.

In some cultures people gesture more than in others, and similar gestures may have different meanings; faces may be inscrutable or openly emotional; some languages may sound loud or harsh; and some people talk all the time, while others make use of silence to transmit messages. Arabs, for example, depend on eye contact to build trust, while Japanese and other Asians feel that too much eye contact is intrusive and rude.

Milee, for example, gave the impression of being shy and passive because she kept her eyes lowered when talking, which caused Harry to feel helpless. "Look at me so I can see what you are saying," he would say. She tried, but it was awkward for her. It also took him years to realize that her smile could mean any number of things: happiness, anger, friendliness, shyness, acceptance, or resignation. It also sometimes meant "no" and was her way of avoiding confrontation.

One of the most frustrating things about nonverbal language is that you can't run to the dictionary to look up meanings; often, it can only be learned by trial and error. Some things can be explained; for example, in Muslim lands, when people cross their legs, showing the sole of the foot, the offense may be pointed out to them and they learn not to repeat it. But other nonverbal signals are more subtle. Although not actually wrong, they send out messages which were not intended and are hard to recognize and correct. Jaime, for example, was baffled by Cassie's accusation that he was "trying to be a Latin lover" with her women friends just because he stood close and looked into their eyes when they were talking. He was doing what came naturally to him, but this behavior wasn't natural to Cassie, unless it implied a sexual intent. For this reason intercultural couples have to be doubly aware (or ask for clarification) of each other's nonverbal communication, and they must be careful that their own is being correctly interpreted.

Mario felt that Deirdre "overreacted" to his booming voice, tensed shoulders, and piercing eyes. She was ready for a fight before she heard his first words. He felt she should know that was just his way (which *intellectually* she did, but her instinctive "he's angry...doesn't love me" reaction came first). He did not understand that her sharp retort was her natural defensive reaction to what she felt was the beginning of a fight...which then *became* a fight when Mario, in turn, reacted to her reaction. Each blamed the other for starting the fight, which neither of them wanted. They were in a vicious circle of miscommunication which, over time, got worse instead of better. Innocent conversations escalated into conflict, which was born less of different ideas and beliefs than of different reactions to the other's ways.

Yvette and Ali, on the other hand, because their cultures were so far apart (French/Kuwaiti) and both spoke a language (English) which was native to neither of them, were used to not automatically understanding each other and frequently declared "time out" to ask for clarification and describe how each other's behavior made them feel. Ali was able to tell Yvette that her use of makeup, her style of dressing, and her French perfume embarrassed him when they were with his family because it gave a message to others which he knew she did not intend. She was able to tell him that his overprotective manner (and sudden exclusion of her from "men's topics," which in his society included work, politics, and philosophy) made her feel inferior and isolated. It wasn't that they didn't have disagreements, but they usually managed to get their points across—carefully, tactfully, and painstakingly—never assuming, always reconfirming: "I don't know if this is what you mean to say, but what I'm hearing is...." They managed because they allowed for their differences and took the time to decode one another's words and actions.

Styles of Communication

Styles of conversing are also different for different people. By styles we mean people's manner of carrying on a conversation, their patterns of speech, behaving, and relating to others. There are no right or wrong styles, simply different styles. They often depend on age, education, and gender. Older people are generally more formal in their manners as well as use of language than are younger ones. Men and women have different concepts of what constitutes a friendly conversation and of how to conduct it. In most cultures women are "more likely to be indirect, and to try to reach agreement by negotiation…[and] often end up appearing deferential and unsure of themselves or of what they want."[5] "Men are more likely [than women] to interrupt their conversational partners…to challenge or dispute statements…[and] to make more declarations of fact or opinion. Some wives resent the 'voice of authority'—not realizing that their husband's assertions may represent a masculine style rather than a sense of superiority."[6]

Styles also vary significantly across cultures. Some cultures are direct, while others have elaborate systems of linguistic courtesy or make use of innuendo and subtlety. Some continually interrupt the other to help a conversation along, while others take turns speaking. Some make extensive use of irony and figures of speech. Some engage in elegant forms of greeting and salutation. Some believe less in the value of the spoken word as a means of expressing thoughts and feelings than do others. Some do not always say what they mean, and others do not always mean what they say.

Mario's style was by turns loud, demonstrative, frank, direct, fast, probing, and aggressive. Deidre's was controlled, subtle, evasive, insistent, discreet, cutting, and conciliatory. Harry's was ponderous, personal, and friendly (informal); full of exaggeration, word play, humor, and slang. Milee's in contrast was reserved, indirect, and detached (formal). She believed in silences whereas he couldn't bear them. When she spoke, her speech pattern tended to be monosyl-

---

[5] Tannen, *That's Not What I Meant*, 126-27.
[6] Aaron T. Beck, *Love Is Never Enough* (New York: Harper & Row, 1989), 105.

labic, high-pitched, and rapid-fire, which Harry read as angry or anxious. She felt some things were better left unsaid, that too much discussion could lead to argument, while he couldn't understand what he couldn't hear. For example, it was hard for her to say aloud, "I love you" or "I don't want...." But for Harry she tried to learn. While these stylistic differences were of course also due to individual tendencies, there is no doubt that the cultures in which they were learned were determinants as well.

Couples who have culturally different styles of communicating feel they are on different levels, "talking to the wind," or passing right by each other. They may also believe that the other is not listening or not caring or perhaps simply not being polite, because their assumptions of what constitutes good manners differ. As Andy Capp, the cartoon figure of Englishman Reggie Smyth, put it, "Culture to that lass is practically anything her crowd does and my crowd doesn't."[7]

The truth is that different styles apply to different people, and true communication between intercultural couples requires that they learn to understand, accept, and accommodate each other's style. It is, however, important that they also learn to accept the fact that they probably will never completely understand the other's state of mind and that the problems will not automatically go away just because they become aware of each other's different style. But becoming aware can help eliminate some of the perplexity and blaming. And the couple might find that over time they even benefit from learning and using each other's style and compensating for each other's blind spots. It takes a lot of work, but the results of the effort are well worth the investment.

---

[7] Reggie Smyth, Andy Capp cartoon in *Washington Post*, 24 April 1984.

17

Responding to Stress and Conflict

> Emotions play a large role in determining not only what we say and how we say it but what we hear. If I am upset, angry or frightened, I will interpret what you say in the light of my own emotional state.
> —Roger Fisher and Scott Brown
> *Getting Together: Building Relationships as We Negotiate*

Just as differences in communication can be a big hurdle in intercultural marriage, so too can culturally different ways of handling stress and/or resolving conflict.

Stress, which is anything pushing us mentally or physically out of kilter, can be caused by external situations such as death, sickness, loss of job, problems with a child, or a marital fight. Change—the birth of a child, a move, a new job, retirement—can also cause stress. The causes of stress may not be of themselves momentous but may be an accumulation of small crises which cause an overload. Sometimes stress is caused by difficulties in dealing with the marital situation itself, in learning to live with another person, especially if the partners approach life and how to live it from very different viewpoints. Whatever the cause, each of us has ways of responding to stress, depending on our age, sex, personality, and cultural or ethnic background. When dealing with life's problems, we tend to go back to our roots, which gives us a sense of comfort and identity. But the ways we choose may be perplexing and upsetting to our partners.

We receive our first lessons on how to cope with life from our parents, from school, and from our peers. Much depends on the kinds of experiences we have on our way to adulthood and how we are taught to react to them. In some cultures, for example, a child learns that it is all right, even healthy, to cry, while in others, crying is shameful or a sign of weakness. One culture may encourage displays of righteous anger, while another teaches self-control. One instructs people to fight for what they want; another believes in passive acceptance of what life brings. In some cultures it is more common for people to eat or drink to relieve stress; in others they pray, shout, or are silent; and in still others, they meditate or talk through their stress—in some cases with step-by-step formulas.

When two people are from the same culture, they can usually comprehend (if not fully agree with or share) each other's way of handling such things as sadness, frustration, anger, grief, worry, loneliness, conflict, illness, or death; they usually know what kind of response is expected. But when they are not from the same or similar background, they may not only be puzzled but upset by the other's behavior and react by interpreting their partner's behavior from their own cultural perspective.

Karen Horney says, "Every culture clings to the belief that its own feelings and drives are the one normal expression of human nature."[1] We judge ourselves (and others) according to our (and their) approximation of what our society considers normal. When these norms differ in a marriage, it is hard to know what to think, how to judge, or how to react to impulsive behavior. One partner may simply not understand what is going on with the other, may interpret the behavior incorrectly, and react to it in a negative or inappropriate way (which in turn may be misinterpreted) until the situation catapults out of control.

> Couples often react to each other as though the other's behavior were a personal attack rather than just a difference rooted in ethnicity. Typically we tolerate differences when we are not under stress. In fact, we find them appealing. However, when stress is added to a system, our toler-

---

[1] Karen Horney, *The Neurotic Personality of Our Time* (New York: W. W. Norton, 1964), 16.

ance for difference diminishes. We become frustrated if we are not understood in ways that fit our wishes and expectations."[2]

Kimberly was brought up in a Jewish-American family where everyone thrived on "letting it all out" and on analyzing every situation ad infinitum. She was, in her words, "nearly driven mad" by her Cambodian husband, Louis, who wouldn't tell her what he was thinking or feeling when they had a disagreement or when he was obviously troubled. Instead he would silently contemplate his fish tanks, oblivious to her attempts to find out what was wrong. He needed to be left alone, to work things out in quiet and solitude. He was afraid that putting his deep emotions into words would cause him to lose control. He not only didn't share Kimberly's tactics but was also agonized by her tears and histrionics.

The way Mehdi (Moroccan) chose to maintain harmony was to avoid dealing directly with things which bothered him, while Daniele (Belgian), by nature and cultural upbringing, thrived on open discussion. For her it was an intellectual pastime as well as an outlet, and she missed the stimulation of locking horns with her husband, who kept his anger inside and tried to smooth things over.

Mario and Deirdre stockpiled resentments and wounds born of their opposing Latin (he usually yelled) and Anglo (she usually became icily soft-voiced) ways of handling stressful situations. Each new conflict brought back past incidents which they had never resolved and triggered reactions resulting from years of misunderstanding and intolerance. Though they had learned to recognize and anticipate one another's coping strategies, they each rejected the other's as unacceptable and were never able either to condone or alter the other's way of handling conflict.

Victor, accustomed in his precise Swiss-German way to accepting pain and grief with silent dignity, was shaken by and disdainful of his Tunisian wife, Zehyra's, theatricality (as he saw it) whenever something went wrong. He began to dismiss real problems as one more case of Middle Eastern dramatics. When her father died, Zehyra's tear-

---

[2] McGoldrick, et al., *Ethnicity and Family Therapy*, 21-22.

ful wailing seemed exaggerated to him, almost insincere. Although he knew her grief was real, her way of expressing it put him off because it was so unlike what he considered a proper display of emotion. He tried to help her get control of herself, which was not at all what she wanted or needed at that moment, and it infuriated her. She saw his reaction as a confirmation of what she felt was his essential coldness and lack of feeling.

The problem is that, although whatever works for the individual is valid, marital partners have to work together to resolve many problems, to negotiate solutions, which means that they have to catch misunderstandings and correct them before they go too far. Not responding "appropriately" is often mistaken for not caring about or not really loving the other, and a kind of hopelessness ("We are just too different") sets in. But with sensitivity to and acceptance of differences in ways of reacting to stress and conflict, couples can learn to work through the difficult times together. For some it takes turning to someone outside the family unit in order to gain the distance necessary to break the negative patterns they have fallen into.

Kimberly and Louis were two who seemed to be stuck in a no-way-out cycle of incomprehension. In desperation, they agreed to get the help of a marriage counselor, who helped them identify their differences and practice making accommodations to them. Kimberly in time learned to slow down and stop probing Louis with nonstop questions designed to force him to open up. In turn, he learned to tell her what he wanted and needed and to let her express her feelings to him. Only then were they able to create an interactive pattern which respected the behaviors of each and provided them with alternate methods of dealing with problems. She learned to appreciate his calm persistence in moments when she was flying off the handle, and he to become more open and spontaneous.

Not that it always worked. Sometimes they fell back into their old habits, which is normal, because when people are under stress, they are not at their best and generally revert to what might be called their original cultural programming. But they knew enough to recognize the patterns and to try again…and again

While some coping styles (and fighting styles) can be complementary, others are conflicting. The important thing is that the couples do not constantly challenge (or belittle) each other's reaction to stress, which will result in a loss of trust in one another and in the conflict-resolution process. By at least identifying and attempting to understand the cultural origin of the partner's behavior under stress, the couple will have a better chance of getting to the source of the problem rather than fighting over their reactions to it.

18

Illness and Suffering

> To each his suff'rings: all are men.
> —Thomas Gray, *In a Distant Prospect of Eton College*

One cause of stress which can be particularly trying for intercultural couples to handle has to do with illness and suffering: How sick is sick? What is healthy? How can illness be prevented? How should it be reacted to? Who should treat it and how?

When a husband and wife come from different cultures, they may have opposing answers to these questions.

McGoldrick, Giordano, and Pearce[1] have stated that people differ across cultures in

1. how they experience pain,

2. what they label as a symptom,

3. how they communicate their pain or symptoms,

4. what their beliefs are about the cause of illness,

5. how they regard helpers (doctors and therapists), and

6. what treatment they desire or expect.

The way people experience and express pain is influenced by culture. In some cultures, the norm or ideal is to suffer silently, while in others one is expected or allowed to be demonstrative and verbal.

What is labeled as a symptom also differs from culture to culture.

---

[1] McGoldrick, et al., *Ethnicity and Family Therapy*, 6-7.

People learn to express symptoms of distress in ways acceptable to others in the same culture. As part of their socialization, they learn that certain complaints of distress are
acceptable and elicit understanding, and that other complaints are unacceptable.... Americans learn that they will
earn more sympathy when they complain about headaches
rather than about memory problems. Mexicans learn that
complaints about memory are acceptable, and the Vietnam-
ese-Chinese learn that complaints about fullness in the head
will be understood by others in their culture.... People in
many cultures are socialized to believe that complaints about
anxieties, worries, and depression are signs of weakness.
These complaints signal to others that people are somehow
sick in the head, and there is far less tolerance for mental
illness than there is for physical illness in many cultures.[2]

Culturally, Fiamma and Andrew exemplify opposite ends of the
spectrum when it comes to communicating their pain and distress.
When Fiamma was expecting their first child, she complained for nine
months and screamed with abandon throughout childbirth in true
Italian style. Andrew, who had opted to be with her when the child
was born (about which she had mixed feelings; she considered childbirth a woman's domain), was torn apart by her expressions of agony
and exhausted by the whole ordeal. Later he was amazed to hear her
describe her child's birth. "It was nothing. Of course I screamed like a
hyena through the whole thing." This was said with a shrug of her
shoulders as if it were the most natural thing in the world. Andrew
could remember his English mother telling his sister at the time of her
birthing, "Keep your mouth shut and remember you're a lady."

Fiamma, on the other hand, never knew when Andrew was sick
because of his stoic British way of keeping silent about his suffering.
She was offended when he turned his back on her loving attempts to
make a fuss over him, taking it as a personal rejection. He, on the
other hand, felt that she was trying to kill him with all the plumping of
pillows, food, and medications rather than allowing him to heal himself in silence and peace.

---

[2] Richard Brislin, *Understanding Culture's Influence on Behavior* (Orlando: Harcourt
Brace, 1993), 332-33

Beliefs about the causes of illness vary according to cultural background and will often dictate treatment. According to some, illness may result from breathing the night air, while others will swear that fresh air is a cure-all. In some cultures, people rigidly adhere to rules of cleanliness as infection preventives, while in others all the fuss about hygiene is regarded as exaggerated nonsense. Some cultural groups believe that illnesses are the result of a curse or spell, or are a punishment for a past evil deed. Illness can be perceived as caused by spirits which must be placated or by one's own carelessness or inattention or by fate, over which one has no control.

Whenever Sune (the Swede) became ill, he was sure it was his own fault; he hadn't taken enough good care of his body and so cured himself by dieting and exercising. His Malaysian wife, Rani, accepted illness and pain as part of what life had in store for her. She was resigned to it and at best turned to a combination of healing herbs and medications for help. Duncan was still influenced by the Christian Science upbringing he had in the United States and ignored telltale symptoms until his pragmatic German wife lost patience and began to take matters into her own hands and design a health and curative regimen which she forced him to follow. She threatened to give him "no more sympathy" until he took care of himself.

Attitudes also vary greatly about doctors and other healers. People from some cultures believe medical professionals are the most qualified to treat illness. In others, people have more faith in spiritualists, traditional healers, or God. Some people run to the doctor at the first sign of fever, while others self-prescribe pills and cures.

The relationship between the healer and the patient differs across cultures as well. While many Americans, for example, prefer full medical disclosure, even in the case of terminal illness, in other cultures such disclosure would be considered heartless and counterproductive, denying the patient the disease-fighting ability that hope provides.

Some couples accept each other's preferences concerning health care providers, but others insist on conforming to their own beliefs. Iranian Mohammed insisted that Adela go to a female rather than a male doctor when she needed one. He himself rarely went to any medical professional. (It was part of his manly pride to be able to handle pain and take care of himself.) Joachim took their son Jorge to the parish priest in Portugal to resolve his bouts of depression, while Sara felt he needed psychological assistance. She ended up going to counseling herself to learn how to deal with the two of them.

Many cultures will not even consider mental health professionals. "Therapists are for crazy people," they maintain, and do not believe in seeking assistance for normal life traumas. It is seen as shameful to be unable to resolve problems alone and a betrayal of the family to discuss personal matters outside of the intimate family unit.

Intercultural couples can also disagree about treatment for their illnesses. Should they buy over-the-counter drugs, bathe in mineral waters, depend on acupuncture or the laying on of hands, use cures handed down through the family, take natural herbs and roots as the Chinese and others have done for centuries, or use no medicines whatsoever?

Old beliefs and rituals still prevail; traditional cures are used instead of, or often together with, modern medical practices. Many educated people have more faith in what family history has proven than in modern medicine. Aside from what the spouses themselves adhere to, the conditions where they live will often have a profound effect on their lives, especially if they live in a country where medical care is difficult to obtain. Sometimes one spouse does not trust the medical practices of the partner's country. Treatment is too aggressive or slipshod, medicines are strange, or prescriptions are handled differently. One American husband complained of always being given suppositories in Italy: "They give me a suppository for a headache, so I imagine I'll get an aspirin for piles." Others feel they have to leave for treatment because the facilities are inadequate.

While couples are young, healthy, and without children, issues of illness often don't arise, but when children are born and need medical attention, or when one of the partners becomes seriously sick, deep-seated traditions and beliefs about illness may surface. Most people feel comfortable with their own culture's medical practices, whether justified or not, and their distrust of others may have a negative effect on the healing process.

19

Ethnocentrism

Cosi é se vi pare (Right you are if you think you are).
—Pirandello

Human beings are perhaps never more frightening than
when they are convinced beyond doubt that they are right.
—Laurens Van der Post, *The Lost World of the Kalahari*

The ability to see the world as one's partner sees it, to understand life
from the other's vantage point, to empathize with this other point of
view, to allow for it and meet it halfway may be the true secret to
overcoming the other obstacles to a successful intercultural marriage.
Lack of this ability may be one of the biggest pitfalls.

How able the partners are to walk in the other's shoes depends
on just how ethnocentric (unalterably convinced of the rightness of
their own ways) they are. Webster defines *ethnocentrism* as "the attitude that one's own group is superior."[1] According to interculturalist
Milton J. Bennett, it is the assumption "that the worldview of one's
own culture is central to all reality."[2]

All of us are ethnocentric to a certain degree, convinced that our
way is the only (or right) way, and we judge others according to their

---

[1] *Merriam-Webster's Collegiate Dictionary*, 10th ed. (Springfield, MA: Merriam-
Webster, 1995).

[2] Milton J. Bennett, "Towards Ethnorelativism: A Developmental Model of Intercultural Sensitivity," in *Education for the Intercultural Experience*, edited by R. Michael
Paige (Yarmouth, ME: Intercultural Press, 1993), 30.

approximation to our way. This is as natural and necessary as breathing. All of us need to be ethnocentric about some things; it gives us stability and consistency and is part of what makes us what we are. The problem with people who are ethnocentric in the extreme is that they are intolerant and inflexible and will probably have a hard time making a relationship work, especially an intercultural relationship.

When two ethnocentric people marry, they are often unwilling to consider that there may be alternate and *equally valid* ways of being and doing things. They are incapable of disconnecting "the notion of difference from the notion of superiority, [of turning] the unfamiliar into a resource rather than a threat."[3] They are like people who are convinced that if they just speak louder, they will finally be understood by someone who speaks another language. They not only disagree with or disparage each other's ways, they often also try to convert the partner to their own. Although the more dominant partner may prevail, something basic is lost, for the only way an intercultural marriage can thrive is for the couple to realize that there are many ways to look at the world and to find a way of living their lives together which is reasonably satisfactory to *both* of them, ideally to create a mélange of the two cultures.

Some people are less ethnocentric by nature than others. People who have been exposed during their formative years to more than one culture, children of different-culture parents, or global nomads who have grown up outside of their parent's homelands usually acknowledge the validity of different styles and beliefs. They may tend toward one over the other, but usually this is after consideration of the alternatives and by conscious choice.

Generally the spouse who lives in the other's country is the one who has managed to develop more than one cultural frame of reference, has learned to be more open and more broad-minded, to acculturate socially. For example, of the two, Jaime was less ethnocentric than Cassie and had to do most of the adjusting. Although he struggled with aspects of life in the United States that went against his grain, he was at least open to trying them. Cassie, however, re-

---

[3] Mary Catherine Bateson, *Peripheral Visions* (New York: Harper Collins, 1994), 233.

sisted anything which was different, and they both knew she probably would never have adjusted to living in Santo Domingo. Although she learned to cook a few of his native dishes and enjoyed most of his friends—as long as they spoke English—and went willingly with him to visit his family, she relaxed only when she was back home with her friends in her own milieu. She had no knowledge of and little curiosity about other cultures.

When expatriate spouses resist adapting to the culture they are living in, they spend a lifetime disconnected and discontented, clinging to the culture of their own ethnic group and viewing the local inhabitants as inferior. Sara, for example, over time and by necessity, learned to acquiesce to many Portuguese patterns, but she did so with a discernible degree of contempt. She never totally overcame her conviction that Portugal would be a better place if the people would just "join the modern world." Although she came to truly enjoy her life there, nothing ever made her alter her feeling of cultural superiority, and she rarely missed a chance to point it out—and then wondered why some of Joachim's friends were so "touchy" and unappreciative of her "constructive suggestions."

Traditionally, women have been more open to compromise than men, more interested in preserving a relationship; they have taken its success as their responsibility and its failure as their fault. Consequently, the woman is generally expected to be the one to make the most adaptations.

New York-born Lynn was convinced that the only way to make her marriage work was to embrace the country and culture of her husband (with, as noted before, the exception of the school system), to submerge herself in it, to stop speaking her own language, to cook Austrian food, and to spend time exclusively with their Austrian friends.

For years this seemed to work and everyone was impressed with how well Lynn had adapted to the life of the country. But the time finally came when she felt she had lost something fundamental to her being, had betrayed her own values. Her sense of her own cultural identity, dormant for years, reemerged and made her dissatisfied with her life, much to the confusion of her husband and son, who had assumed that the Austrian way had become her way and that everyone, including Lynn, was satisfied with the arrangement.

Some cultures are more flexible than others and tolerate alternate patterns of living. Others automatically exclude anything different and isolate the nonconformist. People who marry into a culture which requires conformity must be ready to embrace it totally. In Kenya there was only one acceptable way for a woman in Olu's tribe to behave. If Rashida did not live up to that expectation, she was bad. There was little compromise. Similarly, Mohammed had made it clear to Adela when they decided to marry that she must conform to fundamentalist Islamic culture, even though they lived in the United States. Because her own background had taught her to bow to her husband's will, at least overtly, she agreed; but her life became a struggle, not only to live up to standards not her own, but to deal with trying to repress her own spontaneous way of being as well as her needs and wants.

The ideal situation is when both partners are mature and flexible enough to maintain their independence and individuality and at the same time acknowledge the other's. They accept that both have ethnocentric needs which must be respected and recognize that sometimes the other's ways may even work better. American Kimberly and Cambodian Louis were fascinated by each other's culture and were open enough to admit to blind spots within their own. They were able to overcome some of their innate sense of their own cultural superiority and to try new things and different ways. They benefited from some of their differences. It gave a creative air to their life together.

On the other hand Eva (German) was the personification of extreme ethnocentrism, so much so that she denied the concept entirely. She believed her way was the only way. She had no doubt that others behaved differently "because they didn't know any better." Fortunately, Duncan was easygoing and let her have her way until she intruded on something that really mattered to him. Over the years she learned when it was time to back off. Eventually they found a satisfactory balance: she never lost her sense of "rightness" but conceded that occasionally the *circumstances* demanded a different solution. In that way both saved face.

20

The Expatriate Spouse

Upstairs in my room I listen to Joan Baez records all day and cry. I know how the Sikkimese got their eyes—little damn Mongolian eyes; they damn well cried all the time.
                                                        —Hope Cooke, *Time Change*

The role of the expatriate spouse is not an easy one, no matter how willingly chosen or how second nature it has become, because it is always that: *second* nature, not first. The spouse who will be going to live in the other's country must think seriously about what that might mean—changing from a familiar, comfortable way of life to a new, strange one in which almost everything has to be learned. The expatriate spouse is the one who makes the big sacrifices—family, country, friends, sometimes a profession, often a language.

For the foreign spouse it may mean feeling frustrated with one's own inadequacies or with the difficulties of learning to function effectively in another language, according to other rules and criteria. It usually means coping with different foods, climate, medical practices, housing conditions, laws, standard of living, and political atmosphere as well as conflicting loyalties. It almost always means leaving behind loved ones and supportive friends and starting over, attempting to form new relationships with people who will always be different and who will forever regard the foreigner as different, not quite one of them. Finally, it usually means living with a vague sense of isolation and confusion, of having a double identity. Right alongside a perfectly happy marriage can exist a sense of loss for the identity, the life, or the people left behind. The partner who becomes the expatriate spouse, who has married into the culture with no plans, and perhaps few possibilities of ever returning home except as a visitor, may find that the pressures to acculturate are so strong that adjustment can be extremely difficult.

There are various ways to handle this pressure. One can (1) refuse to adapt and choose instead to reject the partner's culture entirely, continuing to think and act as at home, much like a long-term visitor, (2) let oneself be submerged in the other culture and reject one's own, or (3) blend the two cultures into a new one that validates both (sometimes by behaving one way in one culture and another in the other, other times by moving back and forth between them to fit the demands of the particular situation).

Many who are extremely ethnocentric or have no respect for the other's culture carry on with their lives as though they were still at home: they live in little ghettos, associate only with people of their own country, speak their own language, import their clothes, and cook and eat primarily their own food. Some even pressure the spouse to become a foreigner in his or her own land. Of course, despite their best efforts, some of the other culture rubs off on them.

When Miguel moved to the United States, he did so to please Carol and because the opportunities were better than in his native Chile. But he did everything possible to keep himself separate from the culture of his wife. He made it clear to her that if she wanted to keep him, if she loved him, she would have to help create a little "Chilean haven" in their home. At the same time that he damned the "materialistic, corrupt American culture," he suffered with the struggle of being an outsider and lashed out violently in confusion and frustration. For Carol, Miguel's failure to adjust was also difficult. She felt as though she were living in two countries, that her life was segmented. When she came home from work, the music on the stereo, the language spoken, the cooking aromas in the air, the artifacts decorating the walls, and the rugs on the floor were all distinctly Chilean. Most of the details of their lifestyle were unlike mainstream America, and Carol found herself having to apologize constantly to her foreign husband for "Americanisms" he disdained. She couldn't remember when she had last allowed herself to just "be herself" without fearing his contempt. Miguel put the blame for his unhappiness on those closest to him; thus, the whole family was affected by his depression and alienation.

On the other hand, spouses who try to lose themselves in the other spouse's culture often disclaim their own in doing so. They become "more Roman than the Romans," eating, drinking, dressing, and adhering to all the accepted modes of behavior of the other culture. Some deny their instincts, beliefs, and feelings; they give up their independent sense of self—as Lynn did.

The problem with this kind of immersion is that in the long run, these spouses never quite become part of the other culture, they only become foreigners to themselves. They are like actors who put on costumes and get so caught up in the role they are playing that they lose touch with themselves. They never fully overcome a sense of alienation; they merely add a layer to hide or disguise it. Often these expatriate spouses appear to have adjusted the best, but underneath they are conscious of the falsity of their lives. As Lynn explained it, "One day I woke up with the strangest sense of having lost myself somewhere along the way. Who am I? What do I believe in? I'd lost all sense of my own primary identity and didn't know what I'd become. I didn't belong anywhere anymore."

At the same time, she became aware that the blush was off the romance, that her marriage was no longer the exciting fairy tale she had expected it to be, that she was growing older on foreign turf. She began to question the wisdom of having married Hans and giving up the comfortable regularity of life in the United States, and she didn't know where to turn. She had cut herself off from her old world, from people with her same background who would understand her doubts and dilemmas. Having burned all her bridges, she didn't know how to go forward, and she couldn't go back.

She went through a long period of personal upheaval and discontent, turning her back on many of the Austrian friends she had made and trying to find the American persona she had left behind. She took her bewildered son to meet distant relatives back home and made a point of reconnecting with long-lost friends at her college reunion. She caught up on years of missed books and films from the States. She found work in a real estate agency which catered to foreigners living in Austria.

And then, as suddenly as it had begun, her existential crisis seemed to be over. She suddenly cared less about what others thought of her or how well she fit in. She accepted her outsider status in Austria and learned how to live with it. She understood that she would (or could) not go back to being what she had been before her marriage. She finally learned to be the bicultural person she had become over the years, who just happened to be living in St. Anton.

Adela had also submerged herself in her husband's Islamic culture, if not his country, when she married him, losing her own culture in the process. She described her life as

> living in a constant state of confusion, with no familiar landmarks to help me along. The things I thought I was sure about are constantly challenged in this new world I inhabit, until I begin to question them myself. I get to the point where I'm not sure anymore what is right and what is wrong. I find myself doing things out of character because I think that's how they are supposed to be done. Sometimes I feel as though what is going on around me is not real, as though I were living a movie. I'm never sure what I'm supposed to do or be or what is going to happen next.

Rashida, when she moved back to Kenya with Olu, tried to become "the personification of an African woman" and spoke of the frustration of trying to live according to the norms of her own society and still fit in with her husband's. The cultural definitions of what it meant to be a woman, a wife, and a mother in Kenya were different from those of her own country.

Other spouses manage to adopt what they consider best in the other culture without rejecting or losing their own. They behave according to the demands of the situation. Sometimes they start thinking in two different ways to suit the circumstances. Beneath it all they know who they are and what they believe in, but they can also see value in the host-culture style and the necessity for adapting their own behavior to it. Many of them have two sets of friends: some of the women belong to foreign wives' organizations or women's professional associations, which provide activities and friendships more like those they are familiar with. The men often find comfort in the familiarity of corporate culture. At the same time, they have local friends and associates with whom they do different things and display different behaviors. This was the case for Sara, who by day was Canadian and fretting over her husband's long lunch hour and associating primarily with foreigners and, by night, was Joachim's senhora, living the life of a typical Portuguese matron.

When Yvette moved with Ali to Kuwait, she maintained her own language, religion, clothes, and cuisine in their home. At the same time, she made a point of learning Arabic and following the rules and customs of Kuwait in public. She studied interior design just before coming in order to be able to "do something with myself and escape from the lethargic lifestyle of the privileged women" around her. As a part-time decorator, she preserved a degree of identity, independence, and financial self-sufficiency, which were important to her pride and her sense of self.

One of the problems often faced by expatriate spouses is a lack of professional opportunities commensurate with their training or ability. Many are forced to take low-paying or unsatisfying jobs because of lack of proficiency in the language, work permits, or openings in their field. This is difficult, as professional identity is often a very important part of one's self-concept. Finding suitable substitute activities can be a long process.

Yvette was one of the lucky ones who was able to find a new passion which totally engulfed her. Her interest in the decorative arts led her to become first a collector and then the founder of a small museum of art objects (textiles, pottery, jewelry, etc.) from all over the Islamic world. What began as a hobby became a full-time profession as well as a source of personal satisfaction.

Still, she complained about the strain of living with a double identity, of being the only foreigner in a house full of Arabs, and she talked about the need to go home every so often to "touch base with my own world, to check out my perspectives," and most of all, "to be able to talk to people without having to explain everything." As she said, "the sheer energy required for living in two cultures" wore her down, and she needed to take time out to relax and be herself.

She came close to the ideal: an expatriate spouse who somehow managed to synthesize the various cultures—the one born into, or raised in, and the one married into. This usually takes time, a strong dose of self-esteem, and a positive attitude toward the partner's culture as well as a willingness to continually grow. It also takes a partner who is equally self-confident and appreciative of the "otherness" of the foreign spouse.

Mary and Bill, who met while graduate students at the University of California, were such a couple. Their relationship was one of equals who liked and admired as well as loved each other and who allowed each other to develop within their marriage. Bill was grateful that Mary, who had to make the greatest number of adjustments, was an independent, resilient woman who had her own career, her own identity outside the marriage. Together they withstood the occasional instances of prejudice directed at their interracial marriage. As they pointed out, it is tougher to be in a "visible" intercultural marriage than an "invisible" one. Bill also knew and appreciated that Mary, alone, had to come to terms with the emotional separation from her family and homeland as well as the dilemma of how to enculturate without losing herself, how to be her own person and the summation of all the people within her. This dilemma is perhaps the most continuous one of all, faced by those who cross into another culture as a result of their marriage.

Enculturation without loss of identity is well expressed by another expatriate spouse, writer Ruth Prawer Jhabvala. German-born and English-educated, Jhabvala married an Indian architect and followed him to New Delhi, where she lived for over twenty years.

> To live in India and be at peace, one must to a very considerable extent become Indian and adopt Indian attitudes, habits, beliefs, assume if possible an Indian personality. But how is this possible? And even if it were possible—without cheating oneself—would it be desirable? Should one want to try to become something other than what one is? I don't always say no to this question. Sometimes it seems to me how pleasant it would be to say yes and give in and wear a sari and be meek and accepting and see God in a cow. Other times it seems worthwhile to be defiant and European and—all right, be crushed by one's environment, but all the same have made some attempt to remain standing."[1]

---

[1] Ruth Prawer Jhabvala, *Out of India* (New York: William Morrow, 1985), 21.

21

Coping with Death or Divorce

Nothing endures but change.

—Heraclitus

One important but often ignored aspect of an intercultural marriage is how intercultural couples deal with the end of the marriage, either through death or divorce. Although no one wants to go into a marriage thinking about its end, it is a sad reality that intercultural marriages, just as same-culture ones, do come to an end, sometimes prematurely. Serious thought should be given to "What if?" Being an expatriate spouse is one thing; being an expatriate widow/widower or divorcée/divorcé can be quite another.

The death of a spouse, especially when the marriage was a happy one, is a devastating experience. Although the pain of loss is no greater because the marriage is intercultural, coping with the details resulting from the death of the partner and preparing for one's future are frequently more complicated.

Just as there are culturally different ways of handling pain or stress, so it is with grieving and responding to different customs and superstitions associated with death and burial. All of these may be difficult for the foreign widow or widower to either understand or accept. As anthropologist Mary Catherine Bateson eloquently writes in her book *Peripheral Visions*, "The bereaved is, among other things, a performer in a cultural drama that asserts basic ideas about the nature of life and death and the human heart.... Curiously one does not feel insincere translating words into another language, but translations of behavior come less easily."[1] It may be difficult for the expatriate spouse to publicly exhibit culturally appropriate grieving behavior and, consequently, the spouse may be judged by society as either unmoved or excessively emotional. For the spouse who is left behind, it may also be necessary to adhere to the laws or customs of the land and bow to the influence of the extended family, despite a desire to manage this very personal experience differently.

Although Dorrie was intellectually prepared for the very different customs associated with burials in Japan, when it came time for her to make the arrangements for Hiroshi's cremation, she balked. It was not so much the cremation which she found difficult but the ceremony which followed, when family members transferred the ashes into an urn with chopsticks. She found the whole event emotionally draining and distasteful, but for his family it was an important part of saying good-bye.

For the surviving spouse who is in his or her own land, there may be final directives regarding manner or place of burial of the foreign partner which must be respected. One French woman related the struggle she had with her Iranian brothers-in-law who wanted to take their brother back to Iran for burial. She fought for (and finally succeeded in) having him buried in France close to her and their children. Some widowed spouses relate that they found it particularly hard to endure the final separation symbolized by interring their spouse's body far away in the land of origin. Rosemary found it particularly difficult to fulfill Ravi's wish to have his body returned to India; in a way she saw losing him to the land she had struggled against for her entire marriage as a final blow.

In many countries there are laws specifically regarding widows after their husband's death. For instance, inheritance rights may differ, sometimes depending on whether or not the spouse has taken citizenship in the country. In some lands widows are required to live with the husband's family (sometimes becoming the wife of the brother-in-law—though he may have a wife already). In others, because they are unable or not allowed to work or own property, wid-

---

[1]   Bateson, *Peripheral Visions*, 20.

ows may become financially dependent on their in-laws and subject to their authority. Perhaps even more difficult for the foreign wife is a loss of authority over her children, especially in Muslim countries if she has not converted.

As mentioned before, this was something Mehdi worried about and early on made special arrangements with a trusted friend, another Moroccan married to a foreign woman, naming him as the children's guardian, to assure that Daniele would be protected. From the very beginning, Daniele's mother-in-law had tried to convince her to take steps to secure her financial position and be prepared for the unexpected dangers she would encounter if left alone.

But even in countries in which the laws are not dissimilar to her own, a widow may find that her social standing is largely dependent on her husband and, as a consequence, find herself isolated and alone. Eva, who was in her twenties and quite beautiful when she was widowed, found that she was excluded from "couple functions" in Lima, Peru, at the same time that she was supported and protected by her husband's friends. "Thank God for the help and support of those friends" she said, "but at the same time I was practically forced to become a nun."

Which leads to the all-embracing question—one which is faced by widows and divorcées alike: where do I go now? Eva liked Peru, she had friends there, and she had affordable domestic help with her baby; furthermore, she had cut her ties with her native Germany, where she would have been less restricted, and had no desire to return. In her case the question was resolved with the arrival of Duncan on the scene and her subsequent remarriage. Many widows and divorcees, however, have to find their own answers.

Although divorce or widowhood is easy for neither men nor women, it is perhaps most difficult for the expatriate wives who left their homes and friends, who often gave up promising careers and spent a lifetime as dependents in the husband's country. With the end of the marriage, a feeling of not belonging, of having no ties, no reason to remain in the husband's country sets in. Much depends on how long the couple was married, to what extent the wife had managed to enculturate and find friends, and whether or not there are children. For some of these women the spouse's country has become their own and they would not consider moving. Others remain for the children, either to give continuity with regard to home, school, language, family, and friends or to be near grown children who are settled in their father's country.

But many feel that they have no independent identity in the spouse's country, and despite the fact that they feel like foreigners everywhere, they return home in an attempt to start anew. This is probably more often the case when the marriage has ended in divorce and there is a feeling of needing to escape not only the ex-spouse and his family but also perhaps unfavorable laws regarding custody, child support, alimony, property division, and continued permission to reside in the country.[2]

In divorce, apart from the legal and residential considerations involved, there are also emotional considerations to keep in mind. A relationship does not end just because of divorce; it merely changes. If there are children, the two partners will continue to have a relationship in one form or another. There will usually be financial, educational, health, and often religious issues to be attended to. There may be continued contact with siblings and parents of the ex-spouse. Most important, the children will continue to be a part of the other culture; the rapport with that culture does not end just because the marriage has ended (and the spouse has perhaps moved "back home"). The responsibility and the difficulty of the custodial parent not to deprive his or her children of half of their cultural heritage may be a particular struggle in cases of an acrimonious divorce.

So overwhelming are the problems associated with an intercultural divorce (occasionally accompanied with a sense of shame over what is perceived as failure, especially when the marriage was disapproved of by friends and family in the first place), that many unhappy spouses let their marriages drag on even when they know they should divorce, because they "don't know where to go if it ends." And when it

---

[2] Joy Oliveira Steltzner published a small handbook in 1995, *The International Couples Handbook: A Guide to Critical Issues*, which addresses many of these points and lists addresses of organizations to which international couples might turn for help. Address of Publisher: Insight Out Productions, P.O. Box 16171, Santa Fe, New Mexico 87506.

does end, despite the fact that they may be handicapped in establishing a life of their own or may dislike the country and culture of the ex-spouse, they may have lived there so long that they have lost track of old friends and feel thoroughly out of step with the lifestyle in their homeland. They have burned their bridges and have become marginal to their own culture. The problems, both financial and psychological, of starting out again, finding a new place for themselves, or reinserting themselves in their old world and building a new life are daunting. It often takes more strength and courage to leave than to stay.

No one goes into a marriage thinking about, or wanting to think about, when it is going to end, but certainly the international aspect of the intercultural marriage makes death and divorce something worth giving thought to, sooner rather than later, uncomfortable as that might be.

Part 3

Making Miracles
Isn't Easy

In the preceding sections we have looked at how difficulties emerge for intercultural couples because of the differences in their backgrounds. In this part of this book we change our focus, moving from listing the problems to considering ways of dealing with the differences and ways of predicting more successful relationships, and to offering some things to think about before marriage.

At this point we need to add a note of caution. In this section we are going to concentrate on ways of managing these differences, but we want to make it clear that we certainly don't claim to have all the answers. This is not a recipe or how-to book. Besides, there is no blueprint for success, no one right way. Although some solutions work better than others, ideally speaking, the only right solution is the one that works for each couple. Our ideal solution is only ideal from our point of view; it may be neither possible nor desirable for others. It also may not be feasible in all situations. Many couples report alternating between systems according to the circumstances. Then also, some couples move, over time, from one kind of solution to another.

First we'll outline a few types of intercultural marital models, ways different couples have found for handling their differences within the marital unit. We'll see how the most successful couples first learn about, and then learn to allow for, each other's differentness without losing their own; how they get to know and accept each other as is, not as each would like the other to be. We will see how those couples combine elements of both cultures into their marriages, sometimes sacrificing cherished but nonessential values in the process, to achieve a balance which respects both.

Lest it appear that the couples interviewed could only relate their struggles and conflicts, we will attempt to summarize what most of them considered the strengths or rewards of marrying across cultures, that is, the promises. We will report why, "despite everything," many couples claimed that they "wouldn't have it any other way."

Next we will list the factors to which the couples themselves attribute their successes and show some of the commonalities of those who managed to overcome the more trying times and reap the advantages of their ongoing cultural adventure together.

We will then compile the suggestions the many couples interviewed for this book give to those who might be considering intercultural marriage (or who are at the beginning of their married lives),
along with those of professionals who help couples find their way
through their differences. Finally, in the appendix we will look at particular things intercultural couples can do to learn more about their
partners and their cultural upbringing as well as customs and laws
which they would be wise to look into and take into consideration
before entering an intercultural marriage.

22

Types of Intercultural Marriages

■ Couple   ▨ She   ☐ He

Couples have their own systems for working out the power balance in relationships and for deciding who gives and who takes, whose needs and whose input are given more importance, who is in charge. Some systems are more successful than others because both partners are satisfied with them. This does not mean, however, that the others are failures. Whatever works for the individual couple involved, whether ideal or not, can be considered a functional system. These systems generally fall into one or a combination of (or alternation between) four types of marital models, which we are going to call submission/immersion, obliteration, compromise, and consensus.

Submission/Immersion

The most frequent (and according to many people the most functional) marital model is that in which one partner submits to or immerses him- or herself in the culture of the other partner, almost abandoning or denying his or her own in doing so. Today this is found more in older couples who married twenty to thirty years or more ago, with the partner who immigrated to the other's country doing most of the integrating

To many intercultural couples, the immersion of one partner into the culture of the other is the best and perhaps only way for the marriage to survive, because it reduces cultural conflict. These couples believe that immersion also gives a clear identity to the children of the marriage, making them feel "rooted." Much of the time it is the woman who defers to the man's culture, especially if it is she who either moves to his country, is much younger, or is insecure in her own identity. Even in the most progressive of societies, the main responsibility for the relationship is usually laid at the feet of the woman—it is she who is expected to adapt to the man and his culture. In some cases, especially when the woman is from a male-dominant culture herself, submitting to the man and his culture is the most natural thing for her to do, part of her duty as a wife. However, in these cases the women often keep to their own cultural ways and defend their autonomy in the home or in what they consider the female domain.

Often one partner submits because one culture is so dominant or exclusive that it allows for no alternative. This is especially true in countries in which religion regulates most behaviors. Submission may be merely superficial, however—for public appearance—while in their private life the couple maintains a more balanced relationship. In other situations the personality of one partner may be so dominant that it forces adherence, allowing for little freedom on the part of the other. Often one partner is drawn to and identifies with the other culture (or wants to escape from his or her own) so strongly that it is willingly embraced.

However, despite the many advocates of the submission/immersion model, it has disadvantages. A person is never totally successful at denying or losing his or her ethnic identity though outwardly adhering to another. People cannot stop seeing the world or measuring it according to their own yardstick. They cannot erase the core of their being and, if they try, often find themselves living with contradiction and confusion. They may find themselves outwardly affirming a value which goes against their grain. Frequently, a certain resentment for things which have been sacrificed will emerge (perhaps years later) and eat away at the partner who has lost his or her cultural identity to the other's.

Obliteration

Obliteration refers to the kind of marital model in which couples try to manage their differences by erasing them, by denying their individual cultures altogether. These couples form a new, third-culture identity which has no memories, no traditions, and no cultural causes for conflict. They often give up their languages, lifestyles, customs, and many of their beliefs and values. In a sense they run away from potential conflict.

For some couples this is indeed the only solution because of differences so drastic that there is no alternative. For example, couples who come from historically hostile lands or from different faiths or races may escape to a neutral third country, which they adopt as their own and assume as much of its identity as possible. Sometimes couples meet in a third country, marry, and bring their children up there as natives of that country, far away from the critical eyes of their own families and friends and the rules and customs of their own countries.

Although the advantages are obvious, this is not an ideal solution because it implies a loss for both partners, perhaps willingly accepted in order to be together, but a loss nonetheless.

In the obliteration model both partners have sacrificed and/or lost their ethnic heritage; they have renounced an important part of themselves and denied their children the warmth and richness of their cultures. They are "culture poor," often without any support system or any sense of truly belonging. To quote Austrian artist/poet Friedensreich Hundertwasser, "If we do not honor our past, we lose our future. If we destroy our roots, we cannot grow."[1] Couples may ignore their roots or cut them off by changing their names and re-

---

[1]   From wall of Friedensreich Hundertwasser Haus in Vienna.

jecting their families and social background, but they do so at a terrible price.

Compromise

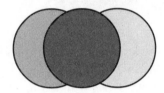

Another way couples may handle their cultural differences is through compromise. In this kind of arrangement, each partner gives up certain (often important) aspects of his or her culturally bound habits and beliefs to make room for those of the other.

Theoretically this is a good solution; it indicates equality, fairness, flexibility, and openness, all of which are essential to the success of intercultural relationships. Nonetheless, compromise means making trade-offs: "We'll bring the girls up Christian and the boys Muslim," for example, or "We'll send money to the Chinese relatives but take our vacations visiting the European ones," or "We'll live in Brazil only till the end of the year and then go back to Italy." There is an adjustment made on the part of both. By its very definition *compromise* means "to adjust or settle [a difference] by mutual concessions."[2]

However, compromise can also mean "to expose to suspicion, discredit"[3]; surrender or give up (one's interests, principles, etc.). And here is the less desirable aspect of compromise in an intercultural marriage: adjustment (or sacrifice) made for the sake of coexistence, which satisfies neither partner. Both have won a little, but both may have lost a little too, and sometimes the values or beliefs which have been compromised really mattered to one or the other of the partners. The Christian who has given up the Christmas tree and all its happy past associations may really begrudge letting go of the tradition. The parent who never speaks his or her language in the home

---

[2] *Merriam-Webster's Collegiate Dictionary*, 10th ed. (Springfield, MA: Merriam Webster, 1995).

[3] Ibid.

may come to feel like an outsider in the family. If this is the case, then no one is really happy. The sacrifice may be greater than the advantage gained. The issues are never really resolved but ready to resurface again and again to be renegotiated or argued over.

For the children also there are issues. They don't know where they belong, and they see parents who may simply be avoiding facing what may be contradictions between the two cultures (or religions). Children are smart; they recognize a "cop-out," parents avoiding rather than resolving major issues.

Many couples, however, consider this compromise type of marital contract better than no give-and-take. Both can claim to have done their part toward making the marriage work. If they keep at it long enough, renegotiating and trying new solutions, they may eventually reach a compromise satisfying to both—which we are calling consensus.

Consensus

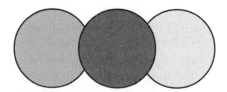

If there is an ideal intercultural marriage model, it is consensus. Consensus is related to compromise in that it implies give-and-take on the part of both partners, but it is different in that it is not a trade-off but an agreement. No scores are kept because the "game" never ends; it is constantly open to revision as circumstances change. The European relatives may suddenly need financial help and the Chinese ones, filial presence; or the job in Italy might fall through and the time in Brazil be extended. In a true marriage of consensus, the partners will go back to the drawing board as often as they need to.

In this ongoing search for solutions, neither partner sacrifices anything essential to his or her well-being. If a solution doesn't work, or they realize that the sacrifice is too great for one or the other, they try a different one. Both are whole people and full partners. They have, or develop, a solid sense of self, of their own differentness, and of their individual needs, principles, and expectations. They continue searching for solutions which work for each individually and for both as a unit. Both are (or become) strong and secure enough in themselves to allow their partners to be different, without considering it a betrayal or a threat. They are able to give to one another, whenever and wherever the need is greatest—even though it may be contrary to the initial agreement—willingly and without keeping count.

The consensus-seeking relationship is a win–win situation in which the issues are worked on until a harmonious resolution is found and both partners emerge with their dignity intact. As Mahatma Gandhi put it, winning is never simply a matter of conquest, "winning requires a transformation of relationships."[4] It also requires creative solutions in which humor, flexibility, and divergent thinking play an important part.

An example of this kind of marriage was provided by Jehan Sadat, widow of the Egyptian leader Anwar Sadat, when she described the intercultural marriage (her mother was British) of her parents.

> My mother really sacrificed herself…she left her country, her family, her friends. She left everything because she loved my father…and she came to my country with different traditions, different customs. And of course she was shocked when she arrived, and she was shocked even later on, until the last moment of her life. She ate the British kind of food. She never touched our kind of cooking. And my father, who was a typical Egyptian man, also never changed his way of life. But what combined them really was love. Love made such a miracle for both of them; it made their lives and their marriage.
>
> My father was Muslim. She was not. She had a great respect for my father…. My father never told her to change her religion, to become Muslim. She never thought of converting, but she was very concerned about us children as Muslims. She used to watch to be sure we fasted during Ramadan. She used to share the fast with us when we were grown up.

---

[4] Taken from Mark Juergensmeyer, *Fighting with Gandhi* (San Francisco: Harper & Row, 1984), 59.

She loved her husband, she loved her Egyptian family,
but at the same time she adored her country.[5]

As Jehan Sadat said, "Love makes miracles," but making miracles isn't easy. It takes time and work and creativity, and it causes stress. People who want their marriage to work must be prepared for this. The couple who will come closest to an ideal intercultural marriage is the one committed to finding a solution which respects both partners; it is the one ready to face the issues, sort them out, or fight them out, over and over again if necessary. To face the pitfalls may be dangerous, but it is the only way to gain the opportunity to fulfill the promises and to grow together in an ever-expanding enriching relationship.[6]

---

[5] Quoted from an article by Prince Michael in *Parade Magazine*, 14 July 1985.
[6] Ideas for this section are based on the concept of *satyagraha* (truth force) as expressed in Juergensmeyer, *Fighting with Gandhi*, 3-11.

23

What about the Promises

In the preceding chapters we have examined at some length the pitfalls of intercultural marriage. "Why ever," one might be tempted to ask, "would anyone want to go into one of these marriages? If there are so many problems and they take so much work, wouldn't it be wiser and more logical to marry within one's own culture? Can all the wise men be wrong who warn against marrying out of your own class and culture?" Remember the Italian proverb cited earlier: "Mogli e buoi, paesi tuoi" (Get your cattle and your wives from your own land).

So why *do* people enter intercultural marriages? What do they get out of them?

Interestingly enough, most of the couples interviewed had a harder time identifying the rewards of their marriages than the problems, perhaps because the positives are more intangible, more out of awareness than the negatives. Many simply answered that they had married because they had fallen in love with someone who just happened to be from another country. They could not differentiate rewards which flowed from the fact that they were from different cultures from rewards that come in any marriage.

Here are the principal rewards they did identify.

1. *Being given the opportunity to increase self-knowledge by being forced to examine and define their own values, ideas, and prejudices, that is, self-growth.* Most of the couples spoke of the difficulties associated with having many of their assumptions and beliefs challenged but acknowledged that in the end,

they were strengthened because of the necessity of having to think things through. They all felt that they were richer, less parochial people because of the experience.

Even couples who finally decided to live apart (Mario and Deirdre, Rashida and Olu) because they were unable to find a compatible modus vivendi felt that the experience of the years they spent together trying to work things through increased their self-knowledge and benefited them as individuals. Lynn, who struggled with her own sense of self while trying to become the ideal Austrian wife and mother, finally realized that transformation wasn't necessary for the success of their marriage and became comfortable in her own skin.

2. *Being exposed to new, different, and valid ways of approaching life and resolving problems.* Even spouses with previous international experience acknowledged that their marriages, because of their very intimate nature, had given them unique opportunities to develop multiple cultural frames of reference from which they could choose how they *wanted* to live their lives. They had been exposed to valid alternatives and discovered the true meaning of cultural relativism.

    Sara and Joachim, as a result of their years of squabbles and soul-searching over their different approaches to life, did a great deal of thinking about their different customs and value systems and learned to tolerate those differences which they were unable to reconcile. "What can't be cured must be endured," Sara conceded.

3. *Experiencing greater variation and vitality in their lifestyle.* Because of exposure to different customs, ceremonies, languages, and countries, most couples felt that they had enriched their daily lives in a way which would probably not have been possible with someone from the same background. They often felt that life with a "foreigner" was more consistently interesting because it was more varied and unpredictable.

    Duncan and Eva were so enthusiastic about their intercultural marriage, with the travel and foreign exposure they had experienced together, that they encouraged their children to seek out their own international partners and were happiest when they were opening their home to a steady parade of guests from other countries and cultures. "Learning your way around the culture of another gives you access to a new way of seeing the world," they maintained, "and keeps life from becoming humdrum."

4. *Developing an international identity.* Many of the spouses talked about enjoying the international identity they acquired through their marriages. They liked the idea of being somewhat out of the ordinary, the center of attention, in both their own and their spouse's country. Obviously, there was a downside in "not belonging," but most felt that their intercultural marriages gave them a cachet which they enjoyed.

Daniele liked standing out in a crowd, being specially treated by everyone, from her Moroccan father-in-law to the traffic official who gave her a speeding ticket. At the same time she was seen as exotic by friends in Belgium with whom she had grown up, envied for her staff of servants and what was seen as a glamourous lifestyle. Hans never gave up his cowboy hat and had an "I ♥ New York" sticker on the bumper of his car, as a way of cementing his identification with the American culture of his wife.

5. *Having children who are bicultural and who have a wider worldview and an ability to be "at home" wherever they find themselves.* The couples who had children felt proud to be the parents of individuals who by the very nature of their dual-cultural exposure would be more broad-minded citizens of the world, cultural mediators, and models for the future.

Dorrie and Hiroshi spoke of their bicultural children: "They grew up with a global worldview and are just naturally sensitive to the nuances of different cultures; I like to think that the world is in their hands—that the time for the true multiculturalist has come, and these kids are born culture-brokers."

6. *Feeling a sense of being pioneers in a new world order.* Some of the couples talked about feeling that through their mar-

riages they were anticipating the future, a world in which cultural, racial, or religious differences would not be a cause for divisiveness. They hoped that their marriages were a sign of the breakdown of ethnocentrism and arbitrary ingroup, outgroup prejudice and misunderstanding which end so often in warfare.

24

Factors for Success

Some intercultural marriages are happier than others. Some falter along the way. Most endure. The strength or weakness of the marital relationship is in the end a personal matter, depending on the two people (not the two cultures) involved. In fact, most couples said that it was more important to be similar in personal values, social class, habits, personality styles, and interests than in the dimensions of culture, race, and religion. Nevertheless, since the differences in their cultural backgrounds often complicated their life together and added extra stress to their relationship, awareness of these differences helped them understand one another better. It prepared them for the inevitability of certain problems and the necessity for dealing with them sensitively in order to live together compatibly. But awareness alone is not enough; there are also certain characteristics which these couples felt were important ingredients in their satisfying intercultural marriages.

Here is a list of these characteristics as seen by the couples. Usually most emphasis was placed on one or two factors which the partners considered essential to their own marriage. For other couples these same things either seemed less important or were difficult to attain. Few of the couples could claim to have all the factors going for them, but the more satisfied partners shared enough of them to keep their marriage on a solid footing while they worked on the others.

1. Commitment to the relationship

2. Ability to communicate

3. Sensitivity to each other's needs

4. A liking for the other's culture
5. Flexibility
6. Solid, positive self-image
7. Love as the main marital motive
8. Common goals
9. Spirit of adventure
10. Sense of humor

Commitment to the Relationship

One thing most couples felt helped them over the bumps was their commitment to the success of the marriage—as well as to each other. Most felt that intercultural spouses try harder than those in mono-cultural marriages, that they not only have a higher degree of toler-ance for differences but also expect from the very beginning that there will be difficulties because of their differences. They believe they are more prepared to make allowances for imperfections or failures than are monocultural couples.

Sometimes their commitment to the marriage is strengthened by pride. Many of these marriages have taken place against the advice of family or friends. The spouses have left the fold and are occasionally disowned or repudiated by their families, or even suspected of being socially deviant. They need to prove to everyone (sometimes them-selves included) that they made the right decision. They don't want to admit that they might have made a mistake—that everyone else might have been right—and face the spoken or implied "I told you so's" back home. So when faced with the prospect of marital breakdown, they have another try at working it out. These same spouses will be quick to acknowledge that a supportive family and an accepting society make the process easier, but, lacking these, they are forced to cling more to one another, which often gives their union extra strength.

There might also be a reluctance to give up the new identity, the uniqueness the couple acquired through the marriage. It's hard to go back to being just like everyone else, especially for those who need to be different, who perhaps were escaping from something they didn't like in their own culture by marrying out of it. Often the same motives which led them into the marriage in the first place keep them working at it when the relationship goes sour.

However, a marriage commitment is not often interpreted similarly by people from different cultures. Some feel that it means an all-inclusive devotion to and responsibility for the well-being of each other, while others consider the first responsibility to be to themselves and leave the relationship to the partner or hope it will somehow take care of itself.

Mohammed thought he was being a good husband by controlling his wife's activities and monitoring her spiritual and physical well-being, and he expected the same kind of devotion from her. Adela's Cuban background had prepared her for dedicating herself to her family, but she had trouble with the all-inclusiveness of the commitment Mohammed expected. For the good of the relationship, she submitted to his wishes, though reluctantly. It wasn't her ideal, but it seemed to be what was necessary to keep the marriage together.

To outsiders, Bill and Mary seemed to be on separate but parallel tracks. Although they shared their dedication to furthering international human rights, each pursued his or her own independent career and dealt with the sacrifices this required on the time they had for each other and their family. At one point Bill adjusted his career track to fit Mary's and followed her to another city because "it was her turn to make the career leap" and because he knew how important this advancement was to her happiness and, consequently, to their happiness.

Massimo and Tove were committed to the bond which united them as they were uprooted time and time again and moved around the world, but they each independently found their own kind of fulfillment. Massimo, when he wasn't working, was squirreled away with his manuscripts, with his nose in his research, or hunched over his laptop computer. He had his circle of friends whom Tove liked but found too "political" for her personal taste. She managed to find clubs and charity work wherever they were posted and kept busy following their children's progress as well as giving the required dinner parties. Both validated the other's activities and enjoyed the variety of their differing interests. Neither felt threatened by the fact that the other looked outside as well as inside the marriage for fulfillment. They didn't feel the need to do everything together to preserve the bond. One point on which, however, they both were vehement was that sexual infidelity would destroy their marriage. It was something neither would tolerate.

The marriage of each couple was based not only on enjoyment of that which was different about the partner and on trust that "otherness" would not divide them, but also on a similar interpretation of the husband and wife roles and the kind of commitment they wanted and expected from one another.

Despite the pulls of their various cultures and perhaps because of the obstacles they had to overcome to be together, most of the couples were more committed to their immediate than to their extended families. This was more natural for some than others, but even those whose cultures dictated total filial devotion and responsibility moved somewhat away from a strict adherence to this rule. They did not necessarily cut themselves off from their extended families, but tended to place more emphasis on the obligations to their own spouse and children.

It was a difficult decision for Ravi to leave India and his family, but he knew that it was necessary for Rosemary's mental health. She was unable to adjust to the all-inclusive Indian concept of family, and if their marriage was to survive, it had to be somewhere else.

Malaysian Rani explained how difficult the choice can be: "When I married Sune (Swedish), I left my family. This is one of the reasons they objected and cried at the time of my marriage; they knew they were losing me more than if I had married someone of my own kind. But it was my own choice and it is my obligation. My marriage has become my homeland; Sune and my children come first."

Ability to Communicate

We have seen in the chapter on language and communication how many obstacles there are to the effective sharing between partners from different cultures, often beginning with the languages they speak and their different styles of behaving and relating. Yet most of the couples cited the ability to communicate as being one of the most essential ingredients of success in marriage, though admitting that it took a lot of "reciprocal translating."

It doesn't seem to matter whether the dominant style of communicating is verbal or nonverbal or whether or not it is peaceful. What is important is managing somehow to understand and be understood by each other. Almost all the more successful couples made an attempt to learn one another's language. They knew intuitively that they could never really know each other unless they learned each other's language. "Translation is a thief" is how Massimo put it. Just grappling with another language expanded their worldview and their ability to perceive and relate. More important, however, they learned one another's style of communicating (of arguing as well as of showing affection) and used it, if not always comfortably, to get their messages across. Both partners were prepared to do their share of reaching out. They were prepared for the perceptual blackouts which occur and were ready to negotiate and try again. Both were committed to succeeding. They agreed to always ask each other for clarification before jumping to conclusions—as Yvette and Ali put it, declaring "time out" to allow for linguistic misunderstanding.

Something few of them actually identified, but which was universally present in the better communicators, was clarity of thought. They themselves knew what they believed and valued and what they wanted to say and so were able to keep trying until they were sure that they had communicated the intended message. Those who were less clear in their own minds, especially regarding what they wanted from the relationship, had a harder time communicating.

Deirdre and Mario, for example, were searching for themselves, unsure of what they really wanted from one another and from their lives, and so they often gave out ambivalent or contradictory messages. In contrast Eva and Duncan, who had both been married before, were more mature and certain about themselves; they knew who they were and what mattered to them and were able to state their minds regarding where they wanted to go with their lives. They learned to probe beneath the surface of one another's words and actions until they knew what they were really disagreeing about. Only in this way could they proceed toward finding a solution.

Cassie and Jaime, despite their very different cultures, personalities, and interests, learned in time to fight for what they wanted and needed from life and from one another. They described themselves as fighting "like cats and dogs" and did not see themselves as effective communicators. But the more they thought about it, the more they realized that although they rarely agreed, at least they had similar methods of fighting. They understood one another and admitted that this was progress. They had come a long way from their early days.

Cristina (Tanzanian) and Stefan (French), who shared internationally mobile childhoods, attributed their success not so much to learning each other's style as to having the courage to open up and talk about hidden chapters from the past which explained present reactions, fears, and feelings. Stefan talked about his unhappy adolescence in a missionary boarding school that turned him against organized religion, which helped Cristina understand why it was useless to try to cajole him into going to church with her. She talked about encounters with racial prejudice and thus gave him some insight into her difficulty in confronting certain social situations as well as her gut reactions to perceived affronts. They learned to be open with one another and to look beneath the surface for an explanation when the other seemed unreasonably inflexible. Their marriage was one of reciprocal learning and teaching.

Certainly not all the couples were born expert communicators. Kimberly and Louis "went through a lot of hell" before they acknowledged their downward spiraling pattern and finally (much to Louis's chagrin and only because Kimberly threatened to leave) went to a few sessions with a couples therapist, where they were made aware of how they were stuck in negative communication patterns which had to be broken before they could develop new relational skills.

Sensitivity to Each Other's Needs

Although this is the third factor on our list, it could easily be the first, because without it a marriage is lifeless. Being sensitive means being able to feel or perceive and respond to outside stimuli, in this case the other's needs, which may be emotional, physical, personal, or cultural. For the intercultural couple, it also means being cross-culturally aware and empathetic. It means learning to understand (if not share) the other's values, beliefs, and needs and comprehending how the other interprets life.

Cristina and Stefan through their open-ended talks about their past experiences learned to understand each other's fears and hurts and to empathize with them, though they could not always agree with how the other handled certain issues. They claimed that this became easier over the years: "Sharing pain as well as joy, a couple merges."

Harry eventually managed not only to understand that Milee was different from his hearty, jovial friends and that she was offended by what she saw as their rudeness and cruel, joking manner, but to actually feel her embarrassment and to suffer for her when someone gave her a big hug. In time he learned to appreciate her need to associate with people from her own country who related to one another in the same way as she did and to support those friendships. Milee, on the other hand, learned to stop seeing Harry as insensitive just because he could not read her thoughts and interpret her nonverbal messages. She learned to know when he needed to hear her speak of her love for him and to explain verbally what she wanted of him as a partner and what she expected from the relationship.

Yvette learned to understand Ali's displeasure when she attracted the attention of men on the street because she was dressed in jeans or other inappropriate Western-style dress and to respect his desire that she conform, at least in public, to the customs of his country. She learned to cater to him with the domestic pampering which he required as an expression of her love. Ali empathized with Yvette's early frustration over her inability to find work in her field, though he himself did not consider a career an important ingredient for a woman's happiness. But when the opportunity came to help her establish her little gallery, he did so willingly because he knew how important it was to her; he knew and accepted that she was not like the women in his country.

In contrast, Olu was never able to understand why his wife couldn't conform to the cultural standards of his people. She struggled constantly with questions of ambivalence in his complicated world and seemed to infuriate him with every protest. He never appreciated the sacrifices she made in her attempts to enculturate and felt that her inability proved her to be an unfit wife. He was never able to step out of his own skin long enough to see what she really wanted and needed; it was too threatening. In the end he divorced her and she returned to the United States.

A Liking for the Other's Culture

It is rarely possible to allow for or accept the other partner's needs if there is a basic dislike of the other's culture. We are products of our cultures, and if our partner disparages our race, nationality, religion, or way of life, an underlying contempt will always separate us. This is not to say that the partners have to like *everything* about each other's culture, but they should like enough of it to be able to accept or over-look the parts they do not.

Miguel liked very little about Carol's American culture. He didn't like its politics; he criticized its work ethic; he found Americans to be rude, classless, money-hungry, and superficial. His dislike prevented him from looking beneath the surface to discover the good qualities or the similarities to his own Chile. His most devastating put-down to his wife was always, "You're acting like a typical American." Carol knew her country was less than perfect, but it was hers to criticize, hers to hate at times, *not his!* She took his criticisms personally, as criticisms of herself—as of course they were in part. His antipathy toward every-thing American and her resentment of that criticism was a constant thorn in their marriage.

On the other hand, Daniele and Mehdi both liked and were at-tracted to the culture of the other. Although both quietly believed in the superiority of most aspects of their own culture, they were open to many aspects of the other.

Daniele loved the exotic beauty of Morocco, her adopted coun-try—the simplicity of life, the kindness and generosity of the people who had gone out of their way to help her adjust to marriage in this new land—and she loved the gentle good manners of her husband. Mehdi was fascinated by European culture, art, and way of life and willingly traveled with his wife to Belgium to visit her family and spend time with her old friends.

Flexibility

Being flexible means being able to adjust, being open to trying something new and different, being willing to consider that there might be a valid alternative to the way one is used to doing or seeing things.

In an intercultural marriage, flexibility is an essential character trait of the successful spouse. Inflexible people are takers: they force the other to do the giving, the changing, the adjusting in marriage. Generally they are insensitive to the other partner's needs and selfish in pursuing their personal goals, insisting that these become their partner's as well. They take themselves too seriously and usually are not much fun.

Being flexible means being like a reed swaying in the wind, bending this way and that according to the circumstances: pliable and strong and able to withstand the strain of sudden changes, unexpected events, or tough times without being uprooted or broken. A satisfying intercultural marriage is made up of two flexible people who learn to take the time and make the effort to understand as much as possible about the other's culture; they are open to trying out different behaviors in their own lifestyle. Flexible couples will be able to tolerate the confusion their two different ways of living bring into their daily routine—especially in the beginning. They will not rigidly adhere to agreements which no longer work but will work through sensitive problems until they find a solution which hurts no one.

When Rosemary and Ravi lived in Canada, Rosemary enjoyed making superficial adjustments to his culture. She wore saris, cooked Indian food on occasion, and studied the language and the art. She was fascinated by the mysticism and the culture of the Indian people. But Ravi made all the really big changes. He adapted to Western ways of socializing, to the Western work ethic and time orientation, and to the Westerner's haphazard neglect of what he considered basic courtesies. He preferred his own ways; he was convinced of their superiority, but he adapted.

When they went to live in India, he expected Rosemary to do the same—to adjust to his ways as he had to hers. But as time passed, both realized that Rosemary was having trouble adapting; she felt she was being asked to give up too much. She missed the privacy of her own home, she had trouble making friends, and she resented the influence of his ever-present family on their domestic lives. She strained under the psychological hardships of living in a land of famine and poverty.

Both finally recognized their limitations and realized the need for another solution, one not based on "his turn, her turn." They were wise enough to know that her inability to adjust to his land had nothing to do with her love for him. Ravi knew that he was going to have to give up a little more of his own culture because he was more able to do so than she was, and he was flexible enough to make another total turnaround in their life together without reproaching her for her failure to adapt.

Fortunately Ravi was able to arrange a posting outside India, this time to West Germany. Once they moved, Rosemary returned to loving all things Indian, to wearing her saris, and to making Indian friends in Bonn (or wherever else they were transferred.) She even taught a course in Indian art to the English-speaking women's club. India was wonderful—so long as she didn't have to live there.

Solid, Positive Self-Image

As we have seen with Rosemary and Ravi, being flexible takes a person with a strong sense of self-worth. People without this sense feel threatened by difference, by nonconformity, and are unable to risk trying something which is not familiar. They want the other partner to be the one who adjusts to *their* familiar and comfortable ways so their security isn't threatened. They also have more trouble admitting that they are wrong.

Most of the people who marry interculturally feel they are, in one way or another, unlike their compatriots who marry people from similar backgrounds. Most of those we interviewed for this book described themselves as different or special in one way or another. Almost all of the spouses, and especially the ones who were in what they themselves considered happy marriages, felt they were not only different but also "above the norm." When they are in fact above the norm, in the sense of having a very positive self-image, they do seem to have a higher rate of success.

"If you don't have a strong sense of who you are, you can get lost in the translation" was how Daniele put it. She had her own business in Brussels when she met Mehdi on a buying trip to Morocco. Mehdi was a physician, the son of a government official, and an intimate of the king. Tove was an only child, bicultural herself and educated in England, the daughter of an international corporate lawyer. Massimo was the eldest in his family, a second-generation member of the respected diplomatic world. Rosemary was the baby, the child who came along many years after the others and was the center of everyone's attention. Ravi was the eldest child and the recipient of a Fulbright Fellowship. Mary was the daughter of a tribal chief as well as a respected academic. Both Eva and Duncan were physically very attractive people. Harry was a successful journalist, and Hiroshi was a distinguished university professor.

All were solid, optimistic people who felt good about themselves and the way they were handling their lives. They approached their international marriage with confidence. They liked their own uniqueness, and they liked the specialness their marriage gave them. They felt that working out a lifestyle with someone from a different background had given them a special self-awareness, but they also knew their limitations and learned to recognize which things were expendable and which were essential to their well-being. They knew who they were and basically were comfortable with themselves.

This is not to say that they were smugly self-satisfied but rather that they had enough self-confidence before marriage to be tolerant of the many ambiguities they encountered and were able to search with their partners for nontraditional solutions to their particular problems. Accepting themselves allowed them to accept the other and to grow together despite, and because of, their differences.

Love as the Main Marital Motive

Love is often the main reason two people marry, and love on the part of both partners—and not only in the passionate or romantic sense—is a necessary ingredient. Insofar as love means that which makes two people want to live together, not just because they are lonely or because being with the other has become a habit, but "for the mutual goal of forming a family to stabilize and improve the quality of their life,"[1] it is a valid motive for marriage. Insofar as it means each spouse wanting to help the partner fulfill him- or herself, love is the best motive for intercultural marriage.

In such a marriage, the emotional energy behind the decision is all-important. If one or both of the spouses enters into the marriage for other reasons, it will most likely be less fulfilling. This is not to say that the marriage won't work if other motives are behind it, but a truly close relationship may be more elusive.

Adela and Mohammed, for example, basically had a marriage fraught with problems. He never accepted her for what she was and wanted her to become a Muslim according to *his* interpretation of the dictates of his faith. He was convinced that it was for her own good, that it was his duty as her husband and religious mentor to insist on his way. He believed he was merely helping her find her best self; but, in actuality, he was denying her the right, the duty, and the opportunity to seek fulfillment in her own way.

Adela, on the other hand, let herself be coerced. She thought she had found the answer to life in Mohammed. She converted to his faith in an honest desire to believe and to find herself, but also to please him, and it was this latter motive that was the strongest.

As time passed, she turned to deceit and trickery to try to get around things she couldn't accept and, at the same time, to avoid confrontation. She subtly tried to dissuade Mohammed from too rigid an adherence to his beliefs. He turned more and more to coercion, and they both lived with a sense of failure as they grew apart in their marriage. A certain sadness and anger always lurked just beneath the surface.

For most intercultural couples married life is a continuous search to find the right balance between what both want for themselves and what both can put up with in the other. Milee and Harry often wondered if they would ever achieve this balance. They saw things *so* differently, it seemed impossible that they would be able to live out

---

[1] W. S. Tseng, J. F. McDermott, and T. W. Maretzki, *Adjustment in Intercultural Marriage* (Honolulu: University of Hawaii Press, 1977), 101.

their lives together without hurting more than helping one another. They explained that what had kept them going was their love for one another, which, like a time-release capsule, kept on aiding them through the hard times until finally they achieved that balance which allowed them to each accept the individuality of the other without undermining the integrity of the relationship.

Common Goals

Whenever both husband and wife want essentially the same things out of life, they will probably find a way to work together toward those ends, despite the difference in their methods of achieving them.

This is a delicate area because it is so closely tied to basic value orientations. But when a couple has developed a similar outlook on where they are going and how they are going to get there, when they have compatible expectations about the kind of life they want, other differences will become less important. Sune and Rani, although from very different cultures (Sweden and Malaysia), had the same ideas about the style of life they wanted: both were avid readers and travelers and liked sharing these things with each other. Neither looked for an active social life; neither felt the need for expensive objects, clothes, or home. They were content with what they had and not ambitious for worldly achievements.

Kimberly and Louis also could not have been more different in their cultural background and orientation. Both, however, felt strongly about one matter: both wanted and needed a solid family unit. Louis had lost his family in Cambodia and Kimberly lost hers through divorce; they were determined that their family would endure. This determination was their driving force, and they hacked away at all the differences and difficulties which threatened them, never losing sight of their primary goal.

A common goal also bound Fiamma, the Italian jet-set leftist, and her English husband, Andrew. Both were dedicated to enabling Andrew to earn lots of money for them to spend in order to establish and maintain themselves in an international circle and keep up their homes in Sardinia, St. Moritz, and London. Values, rules, and obligations were all negotiable in their view, and whatever got in the way of this goal, they eliminated, which included sacrificing some old friends, being together (Andrew traveled eight months out of the year), and associating with her elderly (but socially embarrassing) parents.

While it cannot be said that they were particularly happy people or had an ideal marriage, their dedication to this common goal tied them together. They were not romantic soul mates, but they walked the same path and their marriage endured.

Spirit of Adventure

Part of what makes these spouses the special people they are is another shared characteristic: they either have, or they develop, a spirit of adventure and curiosity about the world.

Almost all of the spouses said they were looking for more out of life than the familiar routine which marrying their own kind would have given them. They didn't intentionally set out to find someone of another culture to marry, but they were open to the idea and ready for the adventure of it when the possibility came their way.

Often they met the foreigners they did because of this very spirit, because they put themselves in a position to meet all kinds of people. Few of them were truly parochial in outlook because, although their previous experiences with people of other cultures varied, their curiosity about the world made them open and adventuresome. Many met while traveling, studying, or working abroad. Others in their own homeland sought out the company of a wider range of people and so met their foreign partners. Many marveled at the twists of destiny which brought them together, but most recognized that their own personalities made it possible.

This spirit that impelled them into their intercultural marriages was not a youthful passing phase. It was something which remained with them during their married lives and helped them confront the unexpected events, the ambiguities, and the sense of unreality which can accompany a cross-cultural existence. This sense of adventure, when coupled with other stable characteristics, served them well through some of the more challenging moments of their marriages.

Ikumi recalled that as a child she always "looked for dares, loved taking risks, was afraid of nothing." As a bride-to-be, she was saddened by but not afraid of the threats made by her parents to keep her from marrying Cecil. This same spirit helped her cross over the double bridge her marriage presented: leaving her family, both physically and spiritually, and stepping into the new and totally different Western culture. It permitted her to follow Cecil willingly to postings around the world, even to some that were not very attractive. It helped her try again, after her near breakdown, when she had to leave Bangladesh and return to her parents' home and beg them to take her in until she was able to regain her health.

Victor had to overcome much of his Swiss-German fastidiousness whenever his Tunisian in-laws visited or when he spent time in their country. It wasn't just the food, but also many of the diverse customs which he found difficult to digest. Actually, he became quite fond of Zehyra's stews, but he never quite managed the goat's eye. Zehyra felt that her marriage was a natural outcome of her personality. She had festered under the oppressive status of women in Tunisia and felt she had improved her way of life by marrying into the Swiss culture. Still, it took time to learn to cope with the new freedoms she found with Victor. Without her spirit of adventure, she would not have been as ready to turn her back on everyone and everything she knew to seek the kind of life she wanted.

None of these adventuresome spouses are boring people; in fact, they all abhor dullness. When they talk about their marriages, they may describe them in many ways: good or bad, difficult or fun, stressful or easy, complicated, unpredictable, and so forth. But they will be quick to add that at least they are never, ever boring.

Sense of Humor

The last factor for success, a sense of humor, is the one most couples agree is important when all else fails; often it is the glue which keeps them together. Yet it is the most culturally bound factor. What makes one person laugh often leaves the other indifferent, confused, or perhaps offended. Almost all of the couples agreed that learning to share laughter, building up a repertoire of funny incidents, and having private jokes were some of the best ways for them to grow closer. Humor was almost always associated with the good times in their marriage, and if the good times outnumbered the bad four to one, their chances for having a successful marriage doubled.

Knowing how to laugh—especially at themselves and at their mistakes as bumbling culture-crossers—takes away some of the tension and gives couples time out to pause and think things through. A humorous interlude helps them remember what binds them together in the midst of their differences. It helps them remember that they entered the marriage not only for all the serious things that attracted them but also because the marriage promised to be fun.

The couples who laughed together also tended to share another characteristic: a sense of optimism regarding their marriage, as if to say: "As long as we can laugh about our weaknesses and difficulties, all is well."

25

Before Taking That Big Step

Hope for the best and prepare for the worst.
                                        —Anonymous

In the preceding chapters we have taken a long and what may appear to be a hard look at intercultural marriage. Although this book is certainly not meant to discourage people from entering what might be the most exciting experience of their lives, it is meant to suggest that intercultural marriage may not be for everyone and that people should take every opportunity beforehand to find out what they are getting into. For most people, these marriages lead to contentment as well as great personal growth. Just learning to live with someone who is different has the potential for increasing understanding and tolerance. For some, however, this intimate intercultural encounter may be a painful and shattering experience. Much depends on the individual's expectations and adaptability as well as, occasionally, outside circumstances which work against the couple.

Being in love alone is not enough to make these marriages work. There are many questions future spouses should ask themselves regarding the state of their own egos and their capacity to cope. There are questions they should also ask the person they love in order to evaluate him or her as a future partner before deciding whether or not intercultural marriage (or intercultural marriage with *that* person) is for them.

Love is blind, it is said. International love is further handicapped because the cultural differences between the two lovers can distort perception. These people have to make a more concerted and conscious effort to know one another by finding out as much as possible about the other's culture and to know themselves by redefining what is and is not necessary for their happiness.

Generally, when two people from different cultures meet and begin to date, they are so busy figuring out the logistics of wooing and winning one another that they may find themselves at the threshold of their wedding without having explored the issues which will turn up in their marriage (the issues discussed in Part 2 as well as some of the legal and financial ramifications of their international union) and the extent of their own compatibility as a couple.

We would like to offer suggestions for prospective spouses before they leap into marriage with someone from another culture. In this chapter we will suggest things the couple can do to learn about one another and about each other's culture. In an appendix we will address external matters which concern international couples and suggest some sources of information.

Things to Do

Experiment with a Trial Run: Live Together

Back in the 1960s, anthropologist Margaret Mead suggested that couples who didn't plan to have children immediately should first make what she called an "individual marriage," a legal tie which was not a lifelong commitment and had no economic consequences should the couple part. Only when they planned on having children should they enter into a legal, lifetime commitment which also included economic provisions for the children in the case of divorce.[1]

Although this theory was shocking when it first appeared, since then many couples have felt that if they live together in a sort of trial run, they will find out how well their personalities and their cultures mesh. It gives the couple a chance to discover how compatible they are and possibly to encounter potential problem areas they might

---

[1] From Fisher, *Anatomy of Love.*

not have thought of otherwise. Possibly for the first time they realize just how tied they each are to many of their own cultural traits and what impact this will have on their day-to-day life together. Living together gives them time and occasion to find answers to many questions regarding such things as neatness, hygiene, and manners; how they eat, treat their friends, define their roles, and handle their finances.

But for any number of reasons, it is neither desirable nor possible for everyone. Living together is not an infallible way to test a relationship because "that little piece of paper" that pronounces a man and woman husband and wife is not merely symbolic; it actually changes the relationship. The new roles and the sense of the permanence of the situation can make previously tolerated traits unbearable, and it can make people change their demands and expectations.

Another problem with this is that frequently one or both of the partners is living in a foreign country, and upon returning home, his or her behavior may radically change—often to the surprise and shock of the other.

Make a Home Visit

Although this may be difficult or impossible in many situations, the best prenuptial preparation for bicultural couples is for each to have an opportunity to live with, or visit for an extended period of time, the future spouse's family before the wedding. Not only will they have an opportunity to see in action the family which molded the partner; they will also have the experience of being immersed in the other's culture. This is especially useful for the man or woman who has been in his or her own homeland during the courtship period or who will possibly be moving to the other country when married. Both will have a chance to see how well the future partner fits in with the other's family and culture.

By living with the family (assuming language is not a barrier), the visitor can see what the family is like without company manners and what customs the family and culture adhere to. This is the time to learn about how decisions are made (and who makes them), how family members relate to one another, how male and female roles are defined, how and to what extent the extended family is included in their lives, how welcome siblings' spouses are made to feel and what their role is, how generations relate to each other, how love and affection are expressed, how arguments are dealt with, how parents punish children, how conflicts are resolved, and how courtesy and respect are displayed. Living with the family will reveal more about how they interact with one another than a thousand discussions.

The visit will also provide a social picture of the family: who their friends are and how they define friendship; how they regard work and handle finances; where and how devoutly they worship; how involved they are in helping others outside the family; what they consider fun; how they entertain; what kind of books they read; whether or not they have pets and how they are treated; what sort of vacations they like; what kind of house or apartment they live in and with what furnishings; and how much or little importance they give (and how they define) such things as cleanliness and hygiene. Finally, an observant guest can gain at least a partial understanding of the family's attitudes regarding education, religion, sex, and marriage. It will be a chance to really focus in on the similarities as well as the differences between the two cultures.

Living with the family will reveal to the prospective spouse the factors that helped form the future partner's character, and it will give a good indication of what patterns of behavior are likely to emerge once they are married and establishing a home of their own.

The spouses who will become expatriates upon marrying benefit the most from living with the other's family, or at least visiting the homeland beforehand, because it provides an opportunity to see how well they can cope with living in the other culture and with being far away from home, family, friends, and familiar support systems. They will also get a feeling for how well they can expect to get along with their future in-laws.

Socialize with the Partner's Friends

Unfortunately, since a home visit to the future spouse's family is an impossible luxury for many, the next best thing is for both people to meet and spend as much time as possible with one another's friends. Couples in love, especially at first, tend to spend all their time alone together. In marriage this isolation usually ends, so it makes sense to get to know one another's friends *before* the wedding, when they can serve as both companions and culture interpreters.

Friends can help these people from different backgrounds learn about one another almost as much as families can. Sometimes people act one way in certain surroundings (because they believe it is what is expected of them) and another way when they are with their own people. An alert culture observer will notice these differences and try to determine what they mean. He or she will see what makes the friends laugh when they are together and what they take seriously, noting how that differs from his or her own group. He or she will also be able to note whether the prospective partner expects to be treated differently when with friends and if the way of interacting between friends or couples is different; if so, that is the time to ask why. Does he or she shy away from any show of affection in public, for example, or display a surprising amount of bossiness? An alert observer can also learn about the friends' attitudes toward religion, morality, dating, marriage, divorce, families, birth control, equality of the sexes, and so on. It is also a good opportunity to discover just what obligations are associated with being a friend in the culture.

If the partner has no same-culture friends at hand, it might be wise to seek out people of the culture in other places. National or ethnic associations or clubs often provide opportunities for meeting couples who can be helpful in showing how social relationships are carried on in the other culture. Here are some of the questions to ask: Do the men have only men friends, and the women, women friends? Do the sexes mix comfortably with one another in open or nonflirtatious ways, and if they do flirt, what are the rules? What do they talk about? Is conversation animated, intellectual, or argumentative, and are there taboo topics? How well is the foreigner accepted among these people and what are their attitudes toward the foreigner's culture or race? And how comfortable are you among them? What do they do together to have fun? How do they entertain? How do they dress? Is the music or way of dancing different? What social graces are important? How do men show courtesy to women, women to men, and both to elders? You can also learn a great deal about communication in the partner's culture. Do people embrace one another; do they stand close or far apart when conversing; how do they use gestures, touching, eye contact, and tone of voice to communicate; how difficult is it for you to participate?

Meeting people, especially friends, from the other culture is an invaluable resource for an intercultural couple. Comparing behavior is also a good way to identify and distinguish personal characteristics of the intended spouse from cultural ones.

A fair rule of thumb: if you fit in with the friends, you will fit in with the culture, and you will have a better than average chance of adapting to one another.

Learn the Language

Knowing the partner's language is important for many reasons. First, communicating with friends and family of the fiancé or fiancée often requires speaking their language. Even if they speak both languages, a knowledge of their language helps you to know them more in depth, to see them at ease in their own language, and to be able to participate in their world more fully. It also circumvents problems of one partner being "left out" when others are around.

Secondly, knowing the language opens up other means of learning about the partner's culture. It permits access to books, magazines, films, and TV programs. It means access to the humor and richness of the spoken language. It also increases the possibility of penetrating the subtleties of the nonverbal language, of learning to recognize the differences in the communication style of the culture in general and the spouse in particular.

Studying the other's language helps each spouse discover what may be different thought patterns of the other culture, in other words, become more interculturally effective. Robert B. Kaplan observed that while English writing and thinking are linear, most Asian languages and thinking are marked by indirection and most Romance languages, by a kind of zigzag.[2] These differences can be disturbing, at least until one becomes aware of the logic behind them.

---

[2]   Robert B. Kaplan, "Cultural Thought Patterns in Inter-Cultural Education," *Language Learning* 16, nos. 1 and 2 (1966).

Most important, learning the language helps the future spouses know one another more completely. Although many spouses spend a lifetime together successfully without knowing the other's language (especially if one partner is fluent in both), not making an effort to learn the language is eliminating one opportunity to know the other more fully, cutting off one source of illumination. Just struggling with a foreign language opens up a new world of understanding and intercultural competency. Not knowing the language is like having a beautiful book, which one loves and cherishes, but can't read.... And that's a pity.

Read and Go to Movies

Those couples with a working knowledge of one another's language can make use of the newspapers, magazines, books, videos, and films of the other's country to learn more about his or her culture.

Future partners can learn a great deal about the internal issues of the country and about its political as well as its social and economic situation from newspapers. They can learn what the problems are, the kinds of crimes committed, the kinds of controls enacted, and the extent of freedom of speech. Are there, for instance, articles critical of the government or military; is there coverage of politically unfavorable events? A lot can be learned by just finding out what is considered news. Newspapers also tell about the lifestyle and interests of the people of the country. An observant reader can find out what the country's attitude is toward his or her own country and how he or she will be looked upon by the natives.

Magazines can serve much the same purpose, but in somewhat more depth. They can reveal the deeper (e.g., political philosophy) as well as the lighter side of the culture: what fads, stars, and sports are popular, how people promote the arts and spend their leisure time. Editorials and advice columns, frequently found in magazines, also give great insight into the popular culture and concerns.

Books serve as indicators of the more lasting character of a people: customs, attitudes, prejudices, problems, morals, beliefs, and values. Books are also an indicator of whether writers and artists are allowed freedom of expression or are censored.

Seeing films or videos about the country, or which were produced there, also helps the prospective spouse learn about the manners, communication style, interests, and living conditions of the people. In films it is possible to *see* what the homes look like, how people dress, what kind of transportation exists, and so forth (at least what the producers want viewers to see).

Study the Religion

If the two people are of different faiths, they should make a point of either taking religious instruction or individually studying each other's faith—even if they do not plan to convert. Especially if they plan to have children, they should be knowledgeable enough regarding each other's faith to respond to inevitable questions regarding conflicting messages and philosophies. Learning about the religion is particularly important if one partner is very devout or if one of the partners is planning to move to the country of the other, where one religion is dominant. Many cultures are deeply involved with the dominant religion, and a study of the history and dictates of the religion is a window on many aspects of the culture, including its values, rules, taboos, ceremonies, and holidays as well as gender roles and limitations. Study of the religion also gives an indication as to whether or not the foreigner will be fully accepted and whether he or she must convert or raise their children in that faith. For couples who are not currently practicing their faith, a study of the religion in which each of them was raised will give valuable insights into each other's formative background and character.

Experience the Cuisine

Potential partners who want to know as much as possible about each other's culture will leave no stone unturned. Cookbooks are treasure boxes of information about ethnic preferences and habits. Seeking out and going to the restaurants which specialize in the partner's cuisine (or better still, eating dinner at a friend's home) is another way to know the people. The smells of the food, the taste, the way the food is eaten, table manners, and, at a restaurant, the interaction between diners and servers all help in the learning process. If the couple is planning to move to one partner's country, the other partner would do well to make sure the food is at least tolerable, if not tasty. Other suggestions include checking out both the bathroom and the kitchen (if possible), seeing how the food is prepared and how much time is involved, and taking note of the decorations on the walls, the music playing, and the table setting. Small details may give hints about the customs, likes, and dislikes of the people.

Search Out Resources

The partner who may be moving to the other's country upon marrying should seek to know as much as possible about that country by using available resources. History books and travel guides are helpful. An article in a major encyclopedia will give substantial background information covering history, climate, economy, population, politics, and other areas of interest. Embassies and various cultural and educational organizations offer extensive selections of printed material about the country.

The prospective spouse's own government probably has an office which deals with the country he or she will be marrying into. The U.S. State Department, for example, has a "country desk" for each nation. The Office of Citizens Consular Services can also provide much of the information regarding the conditions, laws, and customs of the land or can at least tell a future spouse where to go for that information.

The prospective spouse should also seek out people of his or her own country who have lived in the partner's country, people who will be able to pinpoint the differences and the potential difficulties and to give suggestions regarding how to handle the move and adapt successfully. Women should find other women who can tell them what to expect regarding the role of women in the country and possible restrictions. Men should find other men who can tell them about the taboos and duties which might be different from those of their own country. Keep in mind, of course, that no one is neutral; we are all influenced by our own biases.

Another useful thing for these future wives and husbands to find out is whether there is a foreign community of their own nationals in the country they are moving to, or if there are expatriate clubs or associations they could contact before they leave. These groups can provide up-to-date information regarding laws for expatriates as well as unwritten local customs. They can make suggestions regarding what the new spouses should be prepared for, what they should bring with them, whether there is a place of worship for their own faith, and so on. These groups can usually offer information about study and work opportunities, medical assistance, and social activities as well. In other words, they can provide a fairly accurate picture of daily life, information and advice not obtainable in books or official documents.

Foreign wives associations often have newsletters discussing topics of interest or importance from the resident foreigner's point of view as well as listings of activities available to foreigners in that locale. Advice columns, such as "Dear Abby," in the newspapers and magazines are other invaluable resources. They serve to teach social rules to their own people and are filled with tips on culturally appropriate behavior, and they reflect changing mores as well.

Other intercultural couples, especially those with the same backgrounds, can be invaluable resources. But again, the new couple must be alert to distinguish between personal and cultural viewpoints and the possible prejudices which might influence any advice given; all information should be used with discretion. Many couples have joined cross-cultural support or discussion groups and benefited from listening to other couples who have encountered problems and dealt with them in their own style. The new couples found the experience very helpful, for specific suggestions they were able to pick up as well as for the comfort it gave them to know that they were not alone, that others have been in similar situations and survived.

The best resource, of course, is the person's own partner, who has a vested interest in having the loved one make a positive adjustment and be accepted by his or her family and friends. But there are certain things which only women can or will discuss with other women, and men, with other men. There are also aspects of one's own culture which simply don't come to mind or which seem unimportant ("If you want to know about water, don't ask a goldfish," the old saying goes). In any case it is wise to find a confidant or mentor in the other's country who will guide you through the intricacies of behavior, even pointing out gaffes which are often difficult or embarrassing to expose.

Consider Premarital Counseling

Sometimes counseling is very helpful, especially if the couple manages to find someone who is knowledgeable about *cross-cultural* counseling. A good counselor can help the couple examine their motives for the marriage and their expectations regarding life together as well as help them learn how to identify underlying problems and potential points of conflict. A good counselor is one who exposes the cultural aspects of the conflicts, thus depersonalizing them, and at the same time helps the couple find culturally appropriate methods for resolving their differences. With this outside perspective on troubling issues, the couple can become culturally sensitive to each other and can learn to attack the issues, not each other.

Not all cultures, however, are open to this kind of professional help-giving. If that is the case, the couple should seek out a respected older adult, a religious leader, or older friends who can help them identify and deal with specific problems. The important thing here is to find someone knowledgeable about both cultures who can interpret impartially and accurately the partners' mindsets and not be hampered by his or her own cultural biases.

26

Conclusion

For the vision of one person lends not its wings to another person.

—Kahlil Gibran, *The Prophet*

Often a couple feels that they have done just about everything they can to learn about and adapt to each other and the culture into which they will be marrying, or have married but still encounter irreconcilable differences based on cultural values and/or personal needs. They sometimes despair that although they love each other very much, they remain far apart culturally.

It is important to know that even for those who have less than perfect synergy, all is not lost. First, they may be aspiring to an ideal which is more myth than reality. Also, we are not creatures made of stone, but beings in a state of constant change. Although we are made up of elements which are buried deeply in us by our cultural conditioning, we are also continuously evolving and developing in relationship to our current experiences and to the people around us. Intercultural couples over time, living together and loving one another, often begin unconsciously to assimilate characteristics of their partner's culture, to become more alike, and to be more comfortable with and accepting of each other's quirks, all of which eventually blend into the daily life of an intercultural couple.

Growth and change, however, are not always in the direction of blending; sometimes they take a different path. This often worries couples who fear that they may be growing further apart rather than closer. But that may be all right too. There are other ways that marriages can function successfully without being unions of romantic soul mates. Our ultimate separateness is a reality, and intercultural couples, instead of burdening themselves with demands and expectations for a closeness and integration they cannot accomplish or feel, should accept the richness that can come from lives that run parallel but are caring and respectful.

There are some cross-cultural disagreements between couples which go on forever. "We will never see eye to eye on that," they worry. But in fact, these disagreements are often a healthy sign that the couple instinctively knows just how far they can go without damaging something important. Even fights, if they are fair ones in the sense that they are a sign the partners are searching for a solution which works for both, can be good. It is when the spouses give up the fight and give in to or accept something of importance that goes against their nature or integrity, that the individuals as well as the couple are threatened.

Some couples know how to fight constructively; others don't. They see themselves sinking into whirlpools of endless misunderstanding and conflict. But for couples who want to try, there are techniques which can be practiced for improving communication, books one can read on negotiating differences,[1] marital specialists who help cross-cultural couples sort through and identify the true issues and suggest new solutions for recurring problems.

Even when marital partners come to the conclusion that there is not enough to make the continued struggle worthwhile, the marriage does not have to be termed a failure. The experience of living with someone from a different culture, perhaps of raising bicultural children, of expanding one's worldview and ability to tolerate differences is a success in itself. The personal growth one undergoes as a result of the intimate intercultural experience has the potential for producing truly multicultural people—of which the world cannot have too many.

Intercultural couples have chosen a complicated route in life, one which takes more work, more time, more empathy, more honesty—

---

[1] See bibliography.

more everything. They also have an advantage, if they realize this beforehand and decide they are ready to give whatever it takes to make their marriage succeed, never losing track of the fact that in the end they also have the possibility of gaining *more* than couples who didn't dare to be different.

Appendix
Other Practical Considerations

In the main part of the book we have concentrated on how intercultural couples can learn about each other and each other's culture. But there are a few other points the couple should consider and investigate before marrying. We would be remiss if we did not identify some of these issues and suggest sources of information and help.

Laws of the Land

Learning the laws of the land is an important part of preparing for marriage with someone from another country, especially if it is the couple's intention to reside there.

A good place to start is with each partner's own foreign ministry (in the United States, the State Department) and with the embassy or consulate of the country to which they will be moving. Here answers can be obtained to basic inquiries regarding such things as visa requirements, residency restrictions, conditions for legalizing the marriage, and so on. For example, it is not possible for future spouses to visit certain countries until they are actually married.

If the couple is already living in the other country, the expatriate spouse should contact the consular section of his or her own embassy which specializes in citizen services, that is, the section of the embassy which protects the welfare of its own citizens abroad by issuing new passports, for example, and helping stranded citizens return home. It can often furnish the names of international lawyers who can help one learn about the laws which apply to people residing in that country or who marry one of its citizens, or give out a list of organizations whose personnel have the answers to many questions which the future spouses frequently don't know to ask.

As pointed out by Steltzner in *The International Couples Handbook*, there are often differences between what the law allows and what the local practices are. For example, "In Brazil, the 'honor defense'" (which can free a man who kills his adulterous wife) is officially illegal. However, it is still used. In China, laws against checking the sex of a fetus are not enforced and "'sex-selective abortions' are still used to kill female fetuses...."[1]

Citizenship. Does a bride or groom automatically become a citizen upon marrying? If not, can the new spouse apply for official residence immediately after the marriage and for citizenship status later? Does the country permit dual citizenship for adults?

Children's citizenship. Will children be entitled to dual citizenship, and if so, how is it obtained? Will they need two passports? Can they leave the country with one parent without the written permission of the other? Will they be required to enter the armed forces of one or both countries? What restrictions are put upon their citizenship, such as special conditions which must be fulfilled: often countries require that children choose citizenship at age eighteen. Where would the children go if something were to happen to both parents? Are there regulations which would interfere with one or both partners' wishes in this regard? What happens to the children in the case of divorce? Do special custodial limitations apply because one parent is of a different nationality or religion? Are both countries among the thirty-seven nations that have signed The Hague Convention on the Civil Aspects of International Child Abduction (which governs the return of a child to the parent who has been given custody in the case of parental abduction)? In certain countries, a mother can lose her children to the father if her faith is different from the dominant one. What are the legal recourses in such a case? More than one mother

---

[1]   Steltzner, *International Couples Handbook*, 18.

has been known to flee a country and "kidnap" her children when she has been unable to take them out legally.[2] The reverse happens too. Children have been "kidnapped" from the mother's country—though a citizen of it—and taken to the father's, where both are protected by the national laws.[3]

Divorce Does divorce exist in the country where the couple will be living? If so, what are the legal grounds for divorce and the rights of both parents afterward? Under Muslim law, for example, a husband is permitted to divorce his wife without any legal procedure. Such divorce by *talak* merely requires him to state unequivocally three times his intention to repudiate the marriage. Although many countries now require that such a divorce be registered, the wife often has no recourse and in some countries cannot herself seek a divorce. In Morocco, for example, she must have twelve witnesses to her husband's adultery to be able to divorce him.[4]

Other important laws are those regarding alimony, property division, and the continued residence of the divorced foreigner in the country.[5]

Women's rights. Do women have freedom of movement, of dress? Can they be legally (or physically) punished for infidelity or for refusing a husband his conjugal privileges? Can they own property in their own name and sign contracts for themselves? Can they have their own checking accounts? Are they free agents with the same legal rights as their husbands, or are they subject to his authority? In some

---

[2] See Betty Mahmoody, *For the Love of a Child* (New York: St. Martin's Press, 1992).

[3] For information in the United States, contact the Office of Citizens Consular Services, U.S. Department of State, Room 4817, Washington, DC 20520, or The Hague Conference on Private International Law, Permanent Bureau, 6 Scheveningseweg, 2517 KT The Hague, Netherlands.

[4] According to the writings of the Ayatollah Khomeini, a Muslim man or woman may not marry a non-Muslim in continuing marriage; they may be joined only in temporary marriage.

[5] For referrals to foreign lawyers contact the Office of Citizens Consular Services of the U.S. State Department; the International Academy of Matrimonial Lawyers, U.S. Chapter, 211 Congress Street, Suite 40, Boston, MA 02110; the International Legal Defense Counsel, 115 S. 15th Street, Packard Bldg., Philadelphia, PA 19102; or the Family Law Division of the International Bar Association, 6950 North Fairfax Drive, Arlington, VA 22213.

countries a woman cannot drive a car or travel outside the national borders without the written consent of her husband.

Finances and taxation. What are the currency restrictions and taxes and how do they apply to foreign residents or dual citizens? For example, it is not legal to take more than a certain amount of money out of many countries. In other countries income earned or inherited in another country is subject to taxation, sometimes resulting in double taxation.

Ownership of property. Can a foreigner buy, own, and sell property? Can a woman? Can he or she dispose of it freely or is the cosignature of the spouse required? Would a will written in one country apply to properties held in another? Most lawyers agree that it is best to have two wills—for property in each country.

Other regulations. Must a foreign resident register with the police and get a local driver's license and identity card? Is free movement about the country permitted? Are there employment restrictions? Is a special work permit required? What are the laws regarding entitlement to a fair trial and legal representation in case of suspected wrongdoing? How is insurance obtained: medical, life, home, and so forth?

Couples in *Intercultural Marriage: Promises & Pitfalls*

(in order of their introduction)
Yvette (French) and Ali (Kuwaiti)
Duncan (American) and Eva (German)
Hafsa (Moroccan—Mehdi's sister) and Mike (American)
Zoahar (Israeli) and Maria Clotilde (Brazilian)
Hans (Austrian) and Lynn (American)
Esmeralda (Spanish) and a Mexican soccer star
Cassie (American) and Jaime (Santo Domingo)
Cecil (British) and Ikumi (Japanese)
Rashida (African American) and Olu (Kenyan)
Daniele (Belgian) and Mehdi (Moroccan—Hafsa's brother)
Helga (German) and a Libyan
Bill (American) and Mary (Nigerian)
Massimo (Italian) and Tove (Egyptian-Danish)
Cristina (Tanzanian) and Stefan (French)
Milee (Vietnamese) and Harry (Australian)
Dorrie (Dutch-English) and Hiroshi (Japanese)
Deirdre (Irish) and Mario (Italian)
Sune (Swedish) and Rani (Malaysian)
Victor (Swiss) and Zehyra (Tunisian)
Carol (American) and Miguel (Chilean)
Sara (Canadian) and Joachim (Portuguese)
Rosemary (American) and Ravi (Indian)

Fiamma (Italian) and Andrew (English)
Adela (Cuban) and Mohammed (Iranian)
Annamaria (Argentinian) and Erol (Bosnian)
Kimberly (American) and Louis (Cambodian)

Bibliography

Ackerman, Diane. *A Natural History of the Senses*. New York: Vintage Books/Random House, 1991.

Alireza, Marianne. *At the Drop of a Veil*. London: Robert Hale, 1971.

Ashhour, Linda. *Speaking in Tongues*. New York: Simon and Schuster, 1988.

Barbera, Augustin. *Mariages sans Frontieres*. Paris: Editions du Centurion, 1985.

Barron, Milton. *The Blending American: Patterns of Intermarriage*. Chicago: Quadrangle Books, l972.

Barzini, Luigi. *The Italians*. New York: Atheneum, 1964.

Bateson, Mary Catherine. *Peripheral Visions*. New York: Harper Collins, 1994.

Beck, Aaron T. *Love Is Never Enough*. New York: Harper & Row, 1989.

Benedict, Ruth. *Patterns of Culture*. Boston: Houghton Mifflin, 1934.

——. *The Chrysanthemum and the Sword*. Boston: Houghton Mifflin, 1946.

Bennett, Janet M. "Cultural Marginality: Identity Issues in Intercultural Training." In *Education for the Intercultural Experience*, edited by R. Michael Paige. Yarmouth, ME: Intercultural Press, 1993.

Bennett, Milton J. "Towards Ethnorelativism: A Developmental Model of Intercultural Sensitivity." In *Education for the Intercultural Experience*, edited by R. Michael Paige. Yarmouth, ME: Intercultural Press, 1993.

Bode, J. *Different Worlds: Interracial and Cross-Cultural Dating*. New York: Franklin Watts, 1989.

Brislin, Richard. *Understanding Culture's Influence on Behavior*. Orlando, FL: Harcourt Brace, 1993.

Brown, Ursula M. "Black/White Interracial Young Adults: Quest for a Racial Identity." *American Journal of Orthopsychiatrics* 65, no. 1 (January 1995).

Carroll, Raymonde. *Cultural Misunderstandings: The French-American Experience*. Chicago: University of Chicago Press, 1988.

Condon, John C., and Fathi Yousef. *An Introduction to Intercultural Communication*. New York: Macmillan, 1975.

Cottrell, Ann Baker. "Outsiders' Inside View: Western Wives' Experiences in Indian Joint Families." *Journal of Marriage and the Family* (May 1975): 400–07.

——. "Cross-national Marriages: A Review of the Literature." *Journal of Comparative Family Studies* 21, no. 2 (Summer 1990).

Crohn, Joel. *Ethnic Identity and Marriage Conflict: Jews, Italians and Wasps*. New York: Jewish American Committee, 1986.

Devita, Philip R., and James D. Armstrong, eds. *Distant Mirrors: American Foreign Culture*. Belmont, CA: Wadsworth, 1993.

Diekman, John R. *Human Connections*. Englewood Cliffs, NJ: Prentice Hall, 1982.

Doi, Takeo. *The Anatomy of Dependence*. Translated by John Butler. Tokyo: Kodansha, 1973.

Donnan, Hastings. "Mixed Marriage in Comparative Perspective: Gender and Power in Northern Ireland and Pakistan." *Journal of Comparative Family Studies* 21, no. 2 (Summer 1990).

Erickson, Erik H. *Identity, Youth and Crisis*. New York: W. W. Norton, 1968.

Fantini, Alvino, ed. "Introduction—Language, Culture and Worldview: Explaining the Nexus." *International Journal of Intercultural Relations* 19, no. 2 (Spring 1995): 143–53.

Fast, Julius. *Body Language*. London: Souvenir Press, 1978.

Fieg, John P., and John G. Blair. *There Is a Difference*. Washington, DC: Meridian House International, 1975.

Fisher, Helen E. *Anatomy of Love: A Natural History of Mating, Marriage and Why We Stray*. New York: Fawcett Columbine, 1992.

Fisher, Roger, and Scott Brown. *Getting Together: Building Relationships as We Negotiate*. New York: Penguin Books, 1988.

Forer, Lucille. *The Birth Order Factor*. New York: David McKay, 1976.

Goldberg, Milton M. "A Qualification of the Marginal Man Theory." *American Sociological Review* 6 (1941).

Golden, Marita. *Migrations of the Heart*. New York: Ballantine Books: Random House, 1983.

Gornick, Vivian. *In Search of Ali Mahmoud: An American Woman in Egypt*. New York: Saturday Review Press, 1973.

Hall, Edward T. "Learning the Arabs' Silent Language." Reprinted from *Psychology Today*, 1979, in *The Bridge* (Spring 1980).

———. *The Dance of Life*. New York: Anchor Books/Doubleday, 1983.

Harding, Edith, and Philip Riley. *The Bilingual Family: A Handbook for Parents*. New York: Cambridge University Press, 1986.

Ho, Man Keung. *Building a Successful Intermarriage between Religions, Social Classes, Ethnic Groups or Races*. St. Meinrad, IN: St. Meinrad Archabbey, 1984.

———. *Intermarried Couples in Therapy*. Springfield, IL: Charles C. Thomas, 1990.

Hoffman, Eva. *Lost in Translation*. New York: E. P. Dutton, 1989.

Horney, Karen. *The Neurotic Personality of Our Time*. New York: W. W. Norton, 1964.

Ibrahim, Farah A., and David G. Schroeder. "Cross-Cultural Couples Counseling: A Developmental, Psychoeducational Intervention." *Journal of Comparative Family Studies* 21, no. 2 (Summer 1990): 193-205.

Imamura, Anne E. "Husband-Wife Role Misunderstanding: The Case of International Marriage." *International Journal of Sociology of the Family* 16 (Spring 1986): 37-47.

———. "Strangers in a Strange Land: Coping with Marginality in International Marriage." Working paper, University of Michigan, 3 December 1987.

———. "The Loss That Has No Name." *Gender and Society* 2, no. 3 (September 1988): 291-307.

Jhabvala, Ruth Prawer. *Out of India*. New York: William Morrow, 1985.

Johnson, Diane. *LeDivorce*. New York: Dutton (Penguin Books), 1997.

Johnson, Walton R., and Michael D. Warren, eds. *Inside the Mixed Marriage*. Lanham, MD: University Press of America, 1993.

Juergensmeyer, Mark. *Fighting with Gandhi*. San Francisco: Harper & Row, 1984.

Kaplan, Robert B. "Cultural Thought Patterns in Inter-Cultural Education." *Language Learning* 16, nos. 1 and 2 (1966).

Kingston, Maxine Hong. *The Woman Warrior*. New York: Vintage Books/Random House, 1977.

Kluckhohn, Florence R., and Fred L. Strodtbeck. *Variations in Value Orientations*. Evanston, IL: Row and Peterson, 1961.

Kochman, Thomas. *Black and White Styles in Conflict*. Chicago: University of Chicago Press, 1981.

Kohls, L. Robert. *Survival Kit for Overseas Living*. 3d ed. Yarmouth, ME: Intercultural Press, 1996.

Lamb, Patricia Frazer, and Kathryn Joyce Hohlwein. *Touchstones: Letters between Two Women. 1953-1964*. New York: Harper & Row, 1983.

Lederer, William J. *Marital Choices*. New York: W. W. Norton, 1981.

Lee, Daniel B. *Transcultural Marriage: A Study of Marital Adjustment between American Husbands and Korean-born Spouses*. Salt Lake City: University of Utah, Graduate School of Social Work, n.d.

———. "Asian-Born Spouses: Stresses and Coping Patterns." *Military Family* (March-April 1983).

Mace, D. R., and V. Mace. *Marriage East and West*. Garden City, NY: Doubleday, 1960.

Mahmoody, Betty, with William Hoffer. *Not without My Daughter*. New York: St. Martin's Press, 1983.

Mahmoody, Betty, with Arnold D. Dunchock. *For the Love of a Child*. New York: St. Martin's Press, 1992.

Markman, Howard J. "Working with High-Conflict Couples." Paper presented at the Family Therapy Network Symposium, 24 March 1995.

McGoldrick, Monica, Joe Giordano, and John K. Pearce. *Ethnicity and Family Therapy*. New York: Guilford Family Therapy Series, Guilford Press, 1966.

Mead, Margaret. *Male and Female: A Study of the Sexes in a Changing World*. Middlesex, England: Penguin, Pelican, 1950.

Michael, Robert T., John H. Gagnon, Edward O. Laumann, and Gina Kolata. *Sex in America*. Boston: Little Brown, 1994.

Miln, Louise Jordan. *Mr. and Mrs. Sen*. New York: Frederick A. Stokes, 1923.

Morris, Desmond, Peter Collett, Peter Marsh, and Marie O'Shaughnessy. *Gestures*. New York: Stein and Day Publishers, 1979.

Nomoto, Chikaka. "*Amae* in America: Intra- and Intercultural Husband-Wife Relationships." Ph.D. diss., San Diego State University, 1987.

Oldenburg, Don. "In One Ear..." *Washington Post*, 27 February 1987.

Palazzoli, M. S., L. Boscolo, G. Ceccin, and G. Prata, trans. *Paradox and Counterparadox*. New York: Jason Aronson, 1978.

Pedersen, Paul, ed. *Handbook of Cross-Cultural Counseling and Therapy*. Westport, CT: Greenwood Press, 1985.

Pusch, Margaret D., ed. *Multicultural Education: A Cross-Cultural Training Approach*. Yarmouth, ME: Intercultural Press, 1979.

Radasky, Captain R. M. *Ministry Models: Transcultural Counseling and Couples Programs*. Washington, DC: Department of the Navy, 1987.

Rilke, Rainer Maria. *Letters*. New York: W. W. Norton, 1954.

Rosen, Steven. *Future Facts*. New York: Simon and Schuster, 1973.

Sawdey, Michael, ed. *Women in Shadows: A Handbook for Service Providers Working with Asian Wives of U. S. Military Personnel*. La Jolla, CA: National Committee Concerned with Asian Wives of U. S. Servicemen, 1981.

Scarf, Maggie. *Intimate Partners: Problems in Love and Marriage*. New York: Random House, 1987.

Schmitz, Anthony. "The Secret to a Good Marriage." *Health* (March/April 1995).

Seelye, H. Ned, and Jacqueline H. Wasilewski. *Between Cultures: Developing Self-Identity in a World of Diversity*. Lincolnwood, IL: National Textbook, 1996.

Sethi, Robbie Clipper. *The Bride Wore Red*. New York: Bridge Works, 1996.

Shostak, Marjorie. *Nisa: The Life and Words of a !Kung Woman*. New York: Random House, 1981.

Steiner, Shari. *The Female Factor in Western Europe*. Yarmouth, ME: Intercultural Press, 1977.

Steltzner, Joy Oliveira. *The International Couples Handbook: A Guide to Critical Issues*. Santa Fe, NM: Insight Out Productions, 1995.

Stewart, Edward C., and Milton J. Bennett. *American Cultural Patterns: A Cross-Cultural Perspective*. Yarmouth, ME: Intercultural Press, 1991.

Tannen, Deborah. *That's Not What I Meant*. New York: Ballantine Books, 1986.

———. *You Just Don't Understand: Men and Women in Conversation*. New York: William Morrow, 1990.

Telser-Gadow, Barbara. "Intercultural Communication Competence in Intercultural Marriages." Thesis, University of Minnesota, 1992.

Tennov, Dorothy. *Love and Limerence: The Experience of Being in Love*. New York: Stein and Day, 1979.

Ting-Toomey, Stella. "Intimacy Expression in Three Cultures: France, Japan, and the United States." *International Journal of Intercultural Relations* 15, no. 1 (1991): 29–45.

Toffler, Alvin. *Future Shock*. New York: Bantam Books, Random House, 1976.

Tseng, W. S., J. F. McDermott, and T. W. Maretzki. *Adjustment in Intercultural Marriage*. Honolulu: University of Hawaii Press, 1977.

Varro, Gabrielle. *La Femme Transplantee*. Lilles, France: Presses Universitaires de Lille, 1984.

Vosburgh, Miriam G., and Richard N. Juliani. "Contrasts in Ethnic Family Patterns: The Irish and the Italians." *Journal of Comparative Family Studies* 21, no. 2 (Summer 1990).

Werkman, Sidney. *Bringing Up Children Overseas*. New York: Basic Books, 1977.

Wolfgang, Aaron, ed. *Nonverbal Behavior, Perspectives, Applications, Intercultural Insights*. Lewiston, NY: Hogrefe, 1984.